Supporting Language and Literacy

A Handbook
for those who
Assist in Early Years Settings

Suzi Clipson-Boyles

David Fulton Publishers
London

David Fulton Publishers Ltd
2 Barbon Close, London WC1N 3JX

First published in Great Britain by David Fulton Publishers 1996

Note: The right of Suzi Clipson-Boyles to be identified as the author of this work has been asserted by her in accordance with the Copyright, Designs and Patents Act 1988.

British Library Cataloguing in Publication Data

A catalogue record for this book is available from the British Library

ISBN 1–85346–438–4

Typeset by Textype, Typesetters, Cambridge
Printed in Great Britain by Bell and Bain Ltd, Glasgow

Contents

Acknowledgements

Many thanks to all the nursery nurses, learning support assistants, parents and children with whom I have worked and from whom I have learned so much during the years. Particular thanks go to the STA Course students of Oxford Brookes University School of Education who have thrilled me with their knowledge, enthusiasm and thirst for learning, and to John Coe for developing and leading such a splendid course which inspired this book.

Thanks, also, to the adults and children from the following nurseries and schools for allowing me to include their photographs in this book:

Dashwood Road C.P. School, Banbury, Oxon.
Headteacher: Fred Riches

Eynsham C.P.School Nursery, Eynsham, Oxon.
Headteacher: Paul Keates

Foreword

For far too long it was assumed by both teachers and parents that children could learn only when taught by someone qualified to teach in school. That assumption can no longer be held in the light of mounting evidence from research and our experience with children that they learn from everyone and everything in their lives. This is particularly true in the field of language which is always rooted in communication. Children learn as they speak to others, as they write to others, as they read the words of others – the many others, not just those called 'the teacher'.

Experience is the greatest teacher of all and those of us who are proud to be teachers must always remember that our work is most effective when we lead from within and through experience, and that we need to mobilise and bring to the children the talents and energies of all those others who share their lives.

Suzi Clipson-Boyles' book is part of a new wave of publications – much needed as national priorities begin an overdue shift towards the early education of children and a stronger emphasis on literacy, the essential foundation for all later learning. The importance of the teacher's role is reaffirmed yet interpreted in a new way, not condescending or merely informative but in a spirit of partnership. Training is offered to everyone: parents, volunteers in schools, nursery nurses, classroom assistants – in fact all who come alongside children and who cannot then be other than teachers.

Training for partnership with teachers. This surely is a future with so much promise for children.

John Coe
Children Learning: Early Attainment in Reading Project
Canterbury, Christ Church College
May 1996

Introduction

This book is written with educational settings particularly in mind. These include Key Stage One classes, reception classes, nursery classes and nursery schools. It is not the intention of the author to exclude or undervalue the sterling work of other early years settings in which quality learning takes place. Indeed, it is hoped that the book will provide a valuable resource for many of the wide range of people who work with young children. However, because of the limited scope of a book this size, it was considered important to write it with a particular focus.

This focus is on the relationship between language learning and adult support within the context of educational planning, organisation and provision and therefore includes the preparation for and the delivery of the National Curriculum Orders for English. The book considers these government requirements within the wider framework which includes firstly a broader, balanced and integrated curriculum, and secondly the nature of learning. From the very centre of this framework radiates language.

Those who work with children need to understand not only *what* those children are learning about the use of language but also *how* they are learning about language. The quality of support which adults give can have a significant effect upon the quality of learning, but such a responsibility requires guidance. This book aims to offer such guidance as a starting point for developing knowledge, skills and understanding in this most important area of children's progress.

Support staff — a new era Recent years have seen a major sea-change in the nature of the work and the workers in early years educational settings. Teams consist of a much wider range of adults, paid and voluntary, and parents are actively encouraged to become involved in and assist with the work of schools and nurseries, many of them offering help in the classroom on a regular basis. As a result, the teacher's role has developed considerably into that of leader and co-ordinator of other adults in addition to the monitoring, planning and delivery of education to children.

Three other changes have made a notable difference to the profile of early years educational teams. First, the development of National Vocational Qualifications (NVQs) in 1992 as the result of an earlier government White Paper (DE and DES, 1986) have meant that unqualified people now have the opportunity for their work to be monitored, assessed and accredited. This has resulted in a more reflective and developmental approach to work across a range of vocations including child care and education.

Secondly, the commencement, in 1994, of government funding for the training of learning support assistants on courses known as STA courses (Specialist Teacher's Assistant courses) was a further indication of the view that those who work with children need appropriate training if they are to carry out that work effectively. The STA courses aim to extend assistants' understanding of how children learn, particularly in mathematics and English.

Thirdly, there has been a notable increase, in recent years, in the employment of nursery nurses in infant classrooms and schools. As the name implies, the tendency used to be for nursery nurses to work in nurseries. However, the effectiveness of their training and appropriateness of their qualifications in early years care and education have meant that schools are now recognising and valuing their training more than ever before by employing them to assist teachers.

It is not appropriate here to embark upon a political debate about such implications of these changes as pay, conditions, status and professionalism. Nor is it relevant to discuss the pros and cons of diversity in early years provision (although there is no doubt a place for these important discussions elsewhere). However, it is important to state quite clearly that supporting the development of children's language and literacy, in whatever capacity, is an enormous responsibility. The ultimate beneficiaries of adults' competencies are the children and it is to them that we owe a responsibility to work from a sound base of guidance and training.

So who might use this book? It is suitable for private study by individuals who already work with, or would like to support the work of, teachers in early years settings. These might include:

parents
learning support assistants
volunteer reading organisations
school governors.

It is also suitable as a core text for those who are currently in training for such roles. These include:

nursery nurses
specialist teacher's assistants
NVQ participants.

The book could also be used by the group leaders who are responsible for that training. These include:

lecturers in Further Education
lecturers in Higher Education
NVQ assessors
headteachers
INSET co-ordinators.

Finally, it is hoped that the book will also be useful to

teachers
student teachers
playgroup leaders

by giving them guidance on how to maximise the effectiveness of those who work under their supervision.

The term 'assistant' will be used throughout the book to refer to all those who 'assist'. In other words, the term refers to parents, LSAs, nursery nurses, volunteer helpers, students and all others who work under the guidance of early years teachers.

How should the book be used?

This book has been written with a particular emphasis on active learning and reflection by the reader. Wherever possible, the theoretical frameworks are illustrated by practical examples of real situations to be found in early years settings. You are encouraged to relate what is being read to your own direct experience.

Throughout the chapters there are activities which relate to what is being discussed. This is to help you link the theory to practice, to revise what you have read and to use a range of learning processes to digest it. Some of these activities are supported by specially designed activity sheets at the back of the book. Access to children for the purposes of some of these activities will vary according to whether you are currently involved in support work. It is strongly recommended that you arrange visits either through your tutor or independently so that you can develop your learning through direct experiences.

Wherever possible, it is important to try and talk to another person about the activities. This will help you to organise your thoughts, evaluate your work and receive some feedback on your progress. Always try to be positive about the feedback. If it is framed as criticism, try to consider how you can use this in a constructive way to learn something new!

Extending your learning

Clearly, it is impossible to cover every important aspect of such a complex subject as language and literacy. The aim of the book is to stimulate your thinking and awareness, and provide starting points for the development of your practice. The information presented here is only the tip of a very large iceberg. In order to help you take responsibility for extending your own learning beyond the boundaries of this book, an additional reading list is included at the end of each chapter.

Notes to group leaders

The book is designed in such a way that it can also be used by groups. There are suggestions at the end of each chapter on how group leaders and trainers might develop the themes of the chapter in groupwork situations. There are also additional activities which are more suited to collaborative learning.

CHAPTER 1

Working in partnership and teams

This chapter consists of two main parts. The first explores the emergence, meaning and significance of partnership to those who assist in early years settings by examining some of the main dynamics of working relationships. The second part takes a close look at the nature of teams. This is designed to help you understand how complex teams can be, and to reflect upon your own roles and responses within the teams of which you are a member.

Partnership in education

In recent years, the word 'partnership' has become firmly established within the vocabulary of education. The 1988 Education Reform Act has been particularly influential in encouraging the increased involvement of parents and governors in the work of schools, and changes in the training of teachers have resulted in moves towards increased partnership between schools and training institutions. The term is now applied to many of the relationships between those who work in and those who are served by schools and nurseries. The diagram below illustrates some common examples to which the label is currently applied in the everyday language of education.

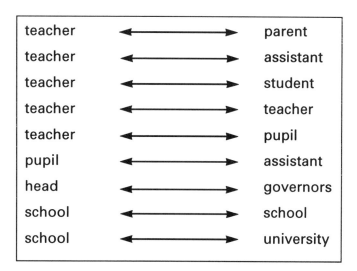

Some examples of two-way partnerships

These examples of partnership are likely to have an agreed, though not necessarily equal, relationship which is beneficial to both parties. Nevertheless, despite the uneven balance of power within some partnerships, the relationship requires shared values and common goals which are reached by a clear commitment to working together. Partnership is most effective where both sides understand each other through clear dialogue, and where decision-making is made through consultation, discussion and honest feedback. Trust is also an important element of partnership, and where all these things are in place a strong and useful bond is usually made.

ACTIVITY 1.1 - Time: 10 minutes

It can be very productive for all of us to reflect on the way we work with others in order to continue developing and improving our performance. What do you consider to be your own roles and responses within your current working relationships? What are the major responsibilities of each individual towards making a partnership work effectively? Make a list of all the different partnerships in which you currently play a part. Do you relate differently in these relationships? Why?

When one works closely with another person in the way that teachers and supporting adults do, it is important to consider the nature of that partnership in order to identify how one's individual contribution affects the success of the working relationship. For example, it is sometimes the case that supporting adults feel reluctant to make suggestions and offer other skills when in fact the teacher would be only too delighted to increase their involvement. By not speaking up, that assistant has deprived the partnership of a valuable opportunity for development. In other words, even if you do not feel you have much power within your working partnership, you do have certain duties, and the ways in which you relate and respond to your 'partner' will have a significant effect on the day-to-day quality of your work.

Those who assist in early years settings can have very different experiences of partnership according to the ethos and policies of the work-place, and the working practices of the teachers. Some teachers give their assistants enormous responsibility and opportunities for decision making whereas others, often for the best of reasons, prefer to keep total control of everything. It is important to remember that, by law, the teacher is accountable for all that happens in her classroom and the head is responsible for all who work in the school. However, despite the fact that, in reality, a sense of equal partnership is rarely felt by classroom assistants, nursery nurses and volunteer parents it is important to remember that true partnership is about common goals rather than equal roles.

ACTIVITY 1.2 - TIME: 30 minutes

Using Sheet 1 on page 72, consider each question in relation to your current working partnership, or one that you have experienced in the past. Do you feel able to share these thoughts with that partner? If not, ask yourself why, and consider whether there is anything which you could do to change this.

Partnership within teams

So far, we have been tending to regard 'partnership' as a two-way relationship, but the meaning of the word has come to mean much more than this. In recent years it has come to represent a particular way of working. In practice, the dynamics of nurseries and schools are complex because they involve groups of people working together rather than simply pairs. When these groups work together in a planned and intentional way they become teams. These teams are therefore mechanisms for partnership.

Teams are interesting animals. They are composed of mixtures of personalities and roles which lead to a complicated set of inter-personal relationships. In order to develop an awareness of how you work within your team, and why, we will now look more closely at some of the important facts about teams.

The value of teams

Imagine eating the ingredients of a Victoria Sandwich, but eating them separately — butter, flour, sugar, raw eggs and sweet jam. Then compare this with eating the cake itself — a miraculous transformation of substances into a different and delicious form. Teams are a bit the same. Each individual member has something different to offer and yet the force of the whole team is so much more than merely the sum total of the individual parts. Indeed, it can have a power and energy of its own which enhances the quality of the work in a most effective way which is beneficial to children and adults alike.

There are many types of teams, and those which exist in early years settings are frequently composed of a wide variety of adults: teacher; nursery nurse; paid assistant; unpaid voluntary assistant; parent; governor; student; play group leader; and special needs support assistant to name the most obvious. Teams also vary in the way they operate — some show real cohesion and solidarity, whereas others harbour the discomfort of resentment and dissatisfaction.

Early years teams operate at their best where all the members have a commitment to the fact that they are a team and really value working together. They hold a shared vision which springs directly from the needs of the children. Other notable features of effective early years teams are:

- clarity of purpose and direction
- clear understanding of roles and responsibilities
- direct and effective communication
- flexibility and adaptability
- early identification of problems and agreed action for solutions
- clear time plans and deadlines
- well-organised systems
- recognition of the team's strengths and weaknesses
- regular self-assessment of how the team is functioning
- meetings which are effective

Team meetings

Regular meetings are essential to the effective communication of any team. The five main purposes of meetings are:

1. To plan for future work.

2. To share information.

3. To identify and solve problems.

4. To make decisions.

5. To maintain a sense of group belonging.

The usefulness of such meetings will depend on the team leader to a certain extent, but it is also the responsibility of all team members to ensure that meetings are productive. Teams in which members merely follow their leader's instructions tend to be less productive than those which share and explore ideas with everyone.

ACTIVITY 1.3 - Time: 10 minutes
Pause to think about the following questions. What role do you take in meetings? How do you contribute to the team? How do you feel about the contributions of others?

Team conflict

All teams can expect to experience conflict sometimes. Conflict is inevitable and it is essential that it should be dealt with rather than avoided. However, the way in which teams deal with the conflict can make a significant difference to the outcome and the future health of the team.

It is important to recognise and acknowledge conflict when it arises, to discuss it and try to understand what is really at the root. One way to start is to identify the areas of agreement and disagreement. This is useful to the team because it creates a better understanding, not only of issues but also of each another.

Exploring conflict can be a creative process. Where a satisfactory solution is the outcome, all the team will benefit from a sense of achievement. This will strengthen the team and create healthy growth as opposed to leaving the area of disagreement in a dark corner where it will lurk and fester.

What makes a good team member?

There is no such thing as a perfect person, and certainly no such person as a perfect team member. We should not all expect to be the same. Just as the cake benefits from different ingredients, so the team benefits from the variety of skills and attitudes which each individual member brings. Nevertheless, it is useful to develop a clear understanding of the general principles towards which we should be aiming when working in teams.

An ideal team member does not follow unquestioningly, merely performing duties and obeying orders. Such passive behaviour does nothing to help the growth and development of a team and its work. Instead, a team member will contribute constructively and creatively in a variety of ways. These are listed below and have been divided into four main sections.

1. Belief system

- is committed to the overall success of the team
- respects the leader but does not expect that leader to take all responsibility

- has high expectations of the team's work

2. Self-awareness

- knows own strengths and skills
- knows own limitations
- recognises areas for development in own practice
- is aware of role within the group
- knows when to ask for help and advice

3. Social skills

- supports the needs of others
- is a good listener
- is aware of impact on others
- does not avoid problems
- is committed to exploring conflict and resolving difficulties
- recognises the importance of open and honest relationships
- respects the feelings of others
- respects different viewpoints
- knows when it is appropriate to speak up
- knows when it is more useful to keep quiet

4. Professional skills

- takes advice constructively
- gives advice constructively
- communicates clearly
- works with and not against others
- thinks creatively
- can demonstrate flexibility
- shares the responsibility of decision-making
- is clear about her role but not inflexible
- can work independently without undermining the work of the team
- reflects and builds continuously on own performance and practice

ACTIVITY 1.4 – TIME: 20 minutes and ongoing
Think about the team in which you work. If you are not currently in post think about your training group. Using Sheet 2 on page 73, tick the boxes which represent areas of competence in your teamwork. Use the unticked boxes as indicators for where you need to plan to develop your skills. Do not overwhelm yourself with too many things all at once. Perhaps take one area of focus each week .

Conclusions

Teams operate effectively where there is a true sense of partnership. Partnership is an ethos, a way of working, a committed relationship between co-operative parties. This way of working involves open dialogue and clarity of purpose shared by all. In early years educational settings the sizes and combinations of teams are varied, but where they work effectively the children benefit from adult support which is built on mutual respect within a co-operative ethos and where the total result is vastly greater than the sum of the parts.

Notes for group leaders

⇨ Discussions about each activity could be carried out in pairs. This would be a safe framework within which to share what may be quite personal thoughts and feelings, rather than opening them up to larger groupwork. Wherever possible, try to precede this with a general discussion about giving peer support or – for example – how one can best help and encourage one's partner through such discussions.

⇨ Group work is very appropriate for examining team skills. Team building activities in groups of four could include:
- building a structure from newspaper to support a wine bottle;
- writing a short story;
- planning a hypothetical party; and
- designing and printing a T-shirt.

⇨ Observing and discussing their roles within the team after the activity is as useful as the team activity itself.

Further reading

Balshaw, M.H. (1991). *Help in the Classroom.* London: David Fulton.
Fox, G. (1993). *Special Needs Assistants – Working in Partnership with Teachers.* London: David Fulton.
Thomas, G. (1992). *Effective Classroom Team-work: Support or Intrusion?* London: Routledge.

CHAPTER 2

The centrality of language in early years settings

This chapter begins with a brief explanation of the National Curriculum requirements for English and Welsh, and then goes on to consider the wider implications of language and literacy in the early years particularly learning, thought and play. It looks at how adults can support these most effectively, and the types of environmental qualities which help to stimulate and develop language and literacy.

How do language and literacy fit into the National Curriculum?

English is one of the three core subjects for the National Curriculum, the other two are Maths and Science. Welsh replaces English as a core subject in Welsh-speaking schools, where English is not a statutory requirement. In Welsh–English-speaking schools, Welsh is studied as a foundation subject in addition to the English core. Both the Welsh and English Orders are divided into three parts called Attainment Targets, one each for oracy, reading and writing.

The Orders for English and Welsh stress the inter-relatedness of these three modes of language and encourages opportunities for learning in this way by making links between the three sections. They also highlight the importance of:

- fluency
- effective communication
- variety of texts
- variety of contexts
- knowledge about language
- Standard English and Welsh
- drama
- media education
- cultural links and heritage

In addition, all other subjects of the National Curriculum have common requirements which stress the importance of competence in speech, reading and writing. Opportunities to use Information Technology are also required across the curriculum (except in Physical Education).

The section of the National Curriculum which relates to the infant Years 1 and 2 is referred to as *Key Stage 1*. At the end of the key stage the children are assessed by external tests plus the teachers' own assessments and their abilities are recorded at the 'Level Descriptions' which most accurately describe their competencies. The average level for a seven-year old at the end of Key Stage 1 is Level 2, but the full range falls between Levels 1 and 3.

The fact that English and Welsh are at the very core of the National Curriculum is an obvious indication of how central our first language is to our learning. Not only is it a subject in its own right, but it also underpins all other areas of the curriculum. There is no statutory requirement to deliver the National Curriculum to reception children, and early years curricula tend to adopt a more integrated approach to learning. However, this broad, balanced and holistic curriculum provided in nursery and reception classes should be providing enriching language and literacy experiences which ensure the continuity of all the developmental processes which have already taken place at home. It is perhaps more educationally sound, therefore, to suggest that such experiences should not be driven by the National Curriculum but should feed into it fruitfully.

Why is language so important?

Language is such an integral part of our lives that we often take it for granted. Every day we engage in hundreds of thousands of complex interactions involving people and texts. But have you ever stopped to think what life would be like without language? No talking, no listening to others talking, no print, no books, no media, no vehicle for expressing our feelings and no framework for our thinking. The reality would be that we would feel extremely isolated from each other and all our ways of working and thinking would be altered and probably reduced.

Language represents the major means of communication between humans and is central to all we do. During the first four years of life, a child learns language at a most incredible rate, at a time when she or he is also learning about the world in which she or he lives. If we are to continue nurturing and extending children's language in early years education it is vital that we recognise and value what each child already knows so that we can plan for their continued development.

There have been several different theories about how language is acquired, but the most recent and significant factor which theorists have identified is that *language learning takes place when children are interacting with adults.* (Wells, 1985.) In everyday life such interactions are numerous and playgroup, nursery or school is only one of the communities within which the child uses language amongst adults. Figure 2.1 illustrates some of the other situations in which language is learned and used.

Each of the situations in Figure 2.1 presents the child with a range of different vocabularies, structures and meanings. The situations can also vary enormously in the ways in which language is used, and most children learn to switch from one to another with remarkable skill.

ACTIVITY 2.1 – Time: 20 minutes
Choose three of the communities from the selection in Figure 2.1 and on Sheet 3 on page 74 record some of the specific features of the language which might take place by thinking about vocabulary and purposes. The purposes can include spoken and written language.

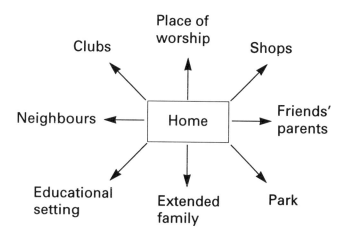

Figure 2.1 Language communities of the child

Language and learning

Language helps children's learning and learning helps children's language. By the age of four, the complexity and fluency of language acquired represents an amazing achievement, especially when we consider how challenging it is as an adult to learn a new language! If we also consider how many other things a four year old knows and understands it becomes clear that a very complex set of processes must be taking place.

To help us identify some of those processes, it is useful to think about the learning of a new language and compare this with the language of the pre-school child. In the secondary school situation, even the most dynamic French teacher can only engage in direct exchange with one pupil at a time. The whole class chanting responses in unison is a technique used to increase the number of responses a pupil can make during a lesson, but what is missing from this type of exchange is spontaneity, individual adjustment and fluency of immediate response. A toddler at home with their primary carer, on the other hand, is engaging in a continuous stream of conversation, backwards and forwards.

Let us look more closely at what might be assisting that toddler with their language development:

- intensive one-to-one interaction
- engaging in a variety of tasks with associated language
- language arising from the child's experiences
- language relating to immediate stimuli
- a range of environments and their associated language
- endless supply of visual resources and artefacts
- stories, rhymes and books

The natural curiosity of young children leads them repeatedly into language learning situations which arise out of normal everyday activities. They are not usually required to wait before they speak as they are in school. Indeed, those who have lived with toddlers will know how continuous and searching their questions can be. The ways in which adults respond to those questions can have a great influence on the development of the child's language. Figure 2.2 illustrates how different responses to the child's questions by the adult can open up or close down the language opportunities for the child.

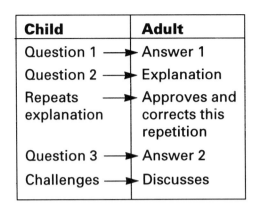

Child	Adult
Question 1 ——→	Answer 1
Question 2 ——→	Explanation
Repeats explanation ——→	Approves and corrects this repetition
Question 3 ——→	Answer 2
Challenges ——→	Discusses

Figure 2.2 Adult engages with the child

In the next figure, however, the adult restricts the flow of subsequent language.

Child	Adult
Question 1——→	Answer
Question 2 ——→	Reprimand

Figure 2.3 Adult disengages with the child

When we compare these two simple examples we can see that the adult in Figure 2.2 has opened up a range of opportunities for the child to use language — in this case five separate units. However, in Figure 2.3 those opportunities have been closed down and the child only utters two units in total. If we multiply the number of child units by the number of times in any day when a child initiates talk we can see that the child in the first example is going to have a vastly different experience to the child in the second example. Let us imagine that a child initiates language with an adult approximately 300 times in one day (this is a conservative estimate). The child in Figure 2.2 is likely to have 5×300 opportunities for talking, a total of 1,500 experiences, whereas the child in Figure 2.3 is only likely to have 2×300, a total of 600 experiences. And these calculations are only for one day.

Of course this is a very false exercise for mathematical purposes and there will always be times when it is not appropriate or easy to develop the conversation fully. Nevertheless, the example is intended to illustrate how significant the role of the adult is in providing opportunities and enabling experimentation and consolidation of young children's language. Where the language is exchanging backwards and forwards between adult and child, the child is hearing language spoken within a specific context. The child can therefore participate and experiment within that context using the language which is being modelled alongside the language they already know.

It is also necessary to consider the quality of the interchange between child and adult. The child in Figure 2.3 is not only experiencing fewer language opportunities, he or she is also experiencing rejection and lack of respect as a learner. Which child do you think is most likely to feel frustrated, unvalued, low learner esteem and possibly rebellious?

Finally, it must not be forgotten that this example is only accounting for the occasions when the child initiates the language. Of course it is quite common for the adult to initiate an exchange, and it is obvious that this adds to the total number of language development opportunities which a child might have in any one day.

ACTIVITY 2.2 – Time: 30 minutes
Using the frameworks in the two figures, write an imaginary script for each, thinking carefully about the sorts of things an adult and child might say in each example. Start each example with the same question in order to explore how it can and cannot be developed. For example:
CHILD: Can I help you to mix that cake, daddy?

Why is language important to children's thinking?

Do you ever talk to yourself when you are on your own? Most people do at some time or other! There will be different reasons for this at different times. Sometimes it might be a response to something or someone ('If he thinks I'm going to get that report done by tonight he's got another think coming!'). Sometimes it might help to organise our thinking ('Now let me see. . . .First I'm going to get those windows washed. That should take till about half past ten. Yes. That should do it. Then I'm going to have a nice cup of coffee!').

Young children can often be observed talking to themselves. The narrative which takes place whilst playing with building bricks, ('Now, I'm going to put two more bricks on there like that and. . . oooops, that was silly. Oh, no! Now they've all fallen down. Oh, no, no, no!'), or the child playing in the water tray, ('Ooooooh! Cold! That's cold, that is. Fill it up. Right to the top. Careful. Careful.'), are externalisations of children's thought processes.

We think in language, and therefore if our language is restricted then so is our thinking. When children are involved in learning experiences, whether these are planned or unexpected, the discussion is actually representing more than conversation. It is, in fact, assisting children with the organisation and extension of thought.

There are many types of thinking. For instance, we think in order to:

- plan ahead
- remember back
- solve problems
- analyse in order to understand
- evaluate critically
- choose a response
- interpret meaning
- create new ideas
- create new meaning
- reflect on experiences

ACTIVITY 2.3 – Time: 10 minutes
Try to think of examples of how you think in each of the ways listed above.

If children are left to their own devices for a large proportion of the time it is easy to see how thinking might not develop to its maximum potential. It is important, therefore, to consider the importance of the relationship between adult and child in order to explore how children's language can be supported in such a way that extends their thinking.

How can adults support and extend children's language?

When we consider the relationship between a pre-school child and its primary carer, the optimum benefits are reaped when that adult responds in particular ways. These include:

- showing an interest in what the child has to say;
- showing respect for what the child knows;
- encouraging the child's own ideas;
- encouraging the child to explain, describe and evaluate;
- demonstrating good models of language;
- correcting through example rather than criticism;
- encouraging the child to experiment with language;
- asking open-ended questions (i.e. which don't just have one correct answer);
- not talking down to or patronising the child;
- demonstrating as they talk;
- listening well to the child;
- drawing attention to texts;
- reading and telling stories;
- talking about stories and books; and
- playing with rhymes.

Once the child joins a larger group of children, the amount of one-to-one interaction with adults is drastically reduced. Collaborative activities where children are learning together offer opportunities for language interaction and these are discussed in detail in Chapter 4. But it is the adult input which is particularly valuable because the adult is able to extend the range of language far more than the child's peers.

This idea of extending within a given range is well documented in the work of Vygotsky (1978). He suggests that adults who support children's learning should extend that learning beyond the child's **current** levels of achievement towards their **potential** levels of achievement. The area of learning between these two levels Vygotsky has called the 'zone of proximal development'. When working only with other children, the child cannot necessarily be extended – in some cases their peers may be restricting their language use because they have not yet reached the same levels. When an adult is present, however, the level of interaction can be influenced in a positive way. Thus, those qualities which are possible for pre-school carers can be successfully adopted by those who work in early years settings when working with groups and individuals.

How does the educational environment influence children's learning?

Children who attend nursery or school for full days are spending a large part of their time in that environment so it is important that it is stimulating and nurturing of children's language, literacy and learning. If children are going to talk they need something worthwhile to talk about. If they are going to learn to read they need interesting and appealing texts. If they are going to learn to write they need opportunities to experiment and practice for real reasons. All these things need to take place in an environment which is supportive and encouraging so that the children develop a confidence in their own abilities and actively seek to learn.

Resources relating to language and literacy will be discussed within the relevant chapters, but it is worth listing here, in more general terms, the types of guidelines which are particularly helpful to the development of children's language and literacy right across the curriculum. The guidelines are:

- good organisation which involves the children
- independence in finding, using and caring for resources
- decision-making opportunities
- time to plan
- time to evaluate
- time to reflect
- experiences which:

    motivate
    build on and extend current knowledge
    challenge
    involve active participation
    involve different types of talk
    have a clear purpose
    require language and literacy in meaningful ways
    are safe
    allow exploration
    allow the children to question
    allow the children to turn to texts
    allow the children to create texts

Children need to value themselves as learners if they are to approach learning positively. They need to be recognised for their achievements and helped to learn through their mistakes. This type of environment cannot be created by displays and resources alone. It is created through attitudes and approaches of the adults in that environment for it is they who can make such a remarkable difference to the quality of children's experiences, learning, welfare and progress.

Language and play

It is a sad fact that even amongst some educationalists the word 'play' is used to describe a recreational alternative to 'work'. ('When you have finished your work you can play in the home corner.') Perhaps the problem lies in the associated meanings of both words, and a lack of clarity about what should actually be defined as 'play' within educational settings.

Enlightened early years teachers know well that with careful planning and preparation, play and work can actually become one and the same thing. Children can learn an enormous amount through play and much of that learning relates directly to language. Play is a complex subject area, and further reading on this subject is highly recommended.

However, just to focus your mind below the surface features of the play activity and into the deeper realms of the language learning that might be taking place, Figure 2.4 illustrates some possible scenarios. Obviously, in the real situation there would be many complex learning processes taking place and many sorts of language. Just one example for each experience has been highlighted here.

Experience	Potential for language and literacy learning
Water play	Concept development through exploration
Puppet play	Exploring language of stories
Home corner	Exploring language of adults
Role play corner	Exploring new vocabulary
Paint play	Use of descriptive language
Clay play	Planning
Multilink	Use of mathematical language

Figure 4.2 Language, literacy and play

ACTIVITY 2.4 – Time: 40 minutes
Carry out three separate 10-minute observations of different individual children engaged in play activities on their own. It is better to catch this spontaneously rather than setting up a false situation. Try to choose three different types of play for each observation. Make three copies of Sheet 4, one for each observation. Later, list on the back of each sheet the learning and thought processes which were indicated by what you saw.

Integrated and discrete experiences

Not only are language and literacy central to everything that happens in early years settings, they are also woven into the very fabric of all other areas of learning. Where language activities take place as part of another area of experience (e.g. topic work on dinosaurs — looking for information) they are referred to as integrated approaches to language. Where language activities take place in their own right (e.g. listening to stories) they are called **discrete** activities.

This chapter has explored language in a particularly integrated way, and indeed an integrated approach to learning and using language is the most natural and meaningful way. However, in order to understand fully the components of language and their implications for supporting adults, Chapters 4 to 8 will examine oracy, reading and writing discretely. However, before turning to these, it is necessary to consider the importance of monitoring children's progress in order to inform our practice and report to teachers. This will be discussed in the next chapter.

Notes for group leaders

⇨ Group discussions about:
  ideas for role play corners
  ideas for displays
  ideas for language games
  language problems encountered
  examples of good practice
  value of National Curriculum
  beyond the National Curriculum
  examples of discrete language activities
  examples of integrated language activities
⇨ Activity 2.1—continue into a whole group discussion about how the structures of language might change according to the different situations.
⇨ Activity 2.2—continue in small groups with a comparison and discussion of the scripts.
⇨ Activity 2.4—develop through a discussion in pairs about the observations.
⇨ In pairs design an interactive display activity on a given theme.
⇨ In pairs plan a play activity with literacy particularly in mind.

Further reading

Bruce, T. (1991). *Time to Play in Early Childhood Education.* London: Hodder & Stoughton.

Hall, N. and Abbott, L. (1991). *Play and the Primary Curriculum.* London: Hodder & Stoughton.

Morris, J. and Mort, L.(1990). *Learning Through Play.* Leamington: Scholastic.

Moyles, J. (1994). *The Excellence of Play.* Milton Keynes: Open University Press.

SCAA, ACAC and TTA (1996). *A Guide to the National. Curriculum* London: HMSO.

Whitehead, M. (1990). *Language and Literacy in the Early Years.* London: Paul Chapman Publishing Ltd.

CHAPTER 3

Observing, recording and reporting

This chapter discusses reasons and methods for assessment and how supporting adults can make useful contributions to the information which teachers are required to compile. This includes observation skills, recording information and reporting back. Self-assessment is also recommended as a tool to help develop reflective and developmental practice.

Individual differences

If all children were predictable in their progress, following the same stages at exactly the same times and responding in identical ways to the same experiences, there would be no need for assessment. Teachers could simply refer to a table of figures and read off the correct level for the child's age. How simple that would be — a production line of identical products!

In reality, of course, children are much more interesting. They are each born with unique genetic profiles and have very different social, emotional and cognitive learning experiences from the day they are born. As a result, they start playgroup, nursery and school not only at different stages of development but bringing with them very diverse sets of attitudes and approaches to learning. If the educational provision in those settings is to be relevant, meaningful and sufficiently challenging for every individual child it is vital that all who work with them fully understand their needs. That understanding comes from careful observation and monitoring and the clear communication of information.

The National Curriculum requires formal assessment at the end of each Key Stage. However, it is the ongoing assessments which provide particularly useful information as these feed directly into planning and provision. Assessments which take place at the end of a period of learning are known as **summative assessments** because they 'sum up' what the child has learned. Assessments which take place during and as part of the continuous process of learning are known as **formative assessments** because they are focusing on the development of learning as it is 'forming'. Those who assist teachers will most likely be involved in the latter.

Adults who have a supporting role in early years settings are not responsible for statutory assessment. However, they do have a valuable part to play in contributing valuable information to the teacher's bank of knowledge. Learning support assistants, for instance, typically spend periods of time daily with children who are finding learning difficult. It is in such a one-to-one or small group situation where there is much information to be gathered; not to make use of the intuitive observations of those adults would be wasting a precious resource which can add to the necessary range of assessment perspectives.

Why is assessment necessary?

Teachers need to assess in order to:

- plan appropriate learning experiences
- measure progress
- identify levels of support needed
- demonstrate school performance
- measure effectiveness of teaching
- inform external agencies
- inform the child
- inform the parents
- inform the next class or school

Who needs to be assessed?

Assessment is not just for children who are experiencing learning difficulties. All children need to have their progress monitored and their needs defined. However, additional diagnostic assessment should also take place for children with particular needs.

Types of assessment

Assessment takes place in different ways for different purposes. These include:

- ongoing assessment
- planned interval assessment
- pupil self-evaluation
- peer evaluations
- observation
- recorded evidence● SATs
- questioning and discussion
- planned outcome
- open-ended outcomes
- standardised tests
- non-standardised tests
- diagnostic tests

Assessment and planning

Sound assessments of children's abilities enable teachers to plan for:
Sequencing – providing experiences in an order which is appropriate and meaningful to the child and which builds on current levels;
Progression – ensuring that the child is moving along a pathway of progress and development;
Differentiation – providing experiences and challenges at varying levels for different groups of children and individuals.

Observation

Observation is a valuable skill to develop. Looking at the end product of a child's efforts (e.g. a piece of writing) often tells us much less than if we have seen the processes through which the child reached that final stage. Observation is about watching and listening.

We can observe children from a distance but we can observe them also whilst we are playing and working with them. However, when evaluating what you have observed it is important to take the following factors into account :

- Did the child know what was expected?

- Was the task planned or unplanned?
- What was the composition of the group?
- Were there equal opportunities for the child to participate?
- What did the child already know and understand?
- What new learning took place?
- What difficulties did the child experience?
- Did the child have access to sufficient appropriate resources?

It would be most unfair to assume that a child is not very competent at cutting out, for instance, when in fact the scissors he or she was using when you observed the child were blunt. In other words, observations need to consider factual information rather than judgemental opinion.

ACTIVITY 3.1 – Time: 5 × 10 minute slots in one week
Make a copy of Sheet 5 on page 76. After preliminary discussions with the teacher choose one child to observe. Ten minutes should be spent in each situation listed on the sheet. Make notes and comments for each about their responses, language, behaviour etc. These might be done at various times across a one-week period. When you have finished collecting your notes, compare them to see what differences there were between the child's responses in the different situations.

Recording

Recording is necessary in order to provide evidence of how the child has progressed over a period of time. Records also help with planning. However, if the records are to be used they need to be useful. They need to be designed in a way which makes the information easily accessible.

Records can be useful for a range of purposes, and the recording format usually varies according to the function of the information. There are long-term profiles of the child which accumulate gradually and include evidence of the child's work. A co-operative approach to this type of record-keeping means that they include a variety of perspectives, including those of the child and parents. This offers a much fuller picture of the child.

Those who assist teachers may also find it useful to make quick records as they work with children in order to be more effective in their reporting back to the teacher. The following checklist provides a reminder of some of the issues involved in recording

- What function is it serving?
- What do I need to record?
- How can I record?
- Is the recording useful?
- Can the records be easily interpreted?
- Who else can record?
- When is it convenient for the teacher to see the records?

ACTIVITY 3.2 – Time: 30 minutes
Imagine that you are working with four children on a group reading activity. Design a sheet which would enable you to record useful information quickly in order to report back to the teacher on the children's reading and responses.

Reporting

Teachers have a statutory responsibility to report information about each child's progress to the parents. Supporting adults have a professional responsibility to report to the following.

(a) The child. As you are working with a child it is important to feed back to them how they are doing in order to encourage and inform;

(b) The teacher. It is highly likely that you will have opportunities to observe certain things which the teacher will not see because she is working with other children at the time. You therefore need to agree with the teacher how and when you will report back after working with particular groups.

Self-assessment and reflection

It is highly beneficial to reflect on what you are doing daily so that you can continue to develop and fine-tune your practice. By observing and critically evaluating yourself at work with children you will become aware of many valuable things and continue to learn in a developmental and constructive way.

ACTIVITY 3.3 – Time: One hour

Make a copy of Sheet 6. After preliminary discussions with the teacher, arrange to tape a session where you are working with a small group of children. Use the sheet to analyse your input to the session. If possible try to discuss the outcomes with another adult, and try to identify three constructive comments which will help you in the future.

Notes for group leaders

⇨ In small groups compare the findings from Activity 3.1.

⇨ In small groups share and evaluate the designs from Activity 3.2.

⇨ Discuss Activity 3.3 with a partner. Try to build in some constructive peer support.

⇨ Bring in examples of *pro forma* for record keeping to compare and discuss.

⇨ In the whole group discuss how often, when and why supporting adults should record information whilst working with children.

Further reading

Barrs, M. and Thomas, A. (Eds) (1988). *The Primary Language Record*. London: CLPE.

Barrs, M. and Thomas, A. (Eds) (1990). *Patterns of Learning. The Primary Language Record and the National Curriculum*. London: CLPE.

DES (1990). *Starting with Quality (The Rumbold Report)*. London: HMSO.

National Primary Centre (1991). *Language Observed*. Oxford: Westminster College.

SCAA (1995). *Consistency in Teacher Assessment: Exemplification of Standards*. London: SCAA Publications.

SEAC (1993). *Children's Work Assessed*. London: HMSO.

CHAPTER 4

The significance of oracy

This chapter explains why oracy is an important and useful part of children's educational development. It examines different types of talk as well as the National Curriculum requirements, and discusses the issues to be considered when preparing for and participating in oracy activities with children.

What is oracy?

Quite simply, the word 'oracy' means speaking and listening. It is the sister word to 'literacy' which means reading and writing. In recent years, oracy has become increasingly acknowledged as an important element of children's learning in addition to the traditionally recognised core of the written word. The National Curriculum Order for English devotes a whole attainment target to speaking and listening which indicates how vital it is to educational provision. Talk is central to our communication process, and language and communication are central to the educational development of children.

Why is oracy so important?

Stop and think how much talking you have done since you woke up this morning. Think about all the different people you have spoken and listened to, how many ways in which you have spoken, and all the different reasons for your talk. When we keep track of our talk it is quite amazing to think of all the thousands of combinations of words, expressions, and nuances which we use almost automatically.

Human talk is an incredible tool for communication and is a central part of how we think, learn and socialise. These four elements — communication, thinking, socialistaion and learning — have been illustrated in Figure 4.1 below in order to highlight the importance of talk in early years educational settings. The diagram is designed to illustrate how oracy lies at the centre of these vital processes. It also shows the ways in which each of these processes operate in many directions between each other via oracy. Each of the four can feed into any other via the 'oracy box'.

ACTIVITY 4.1 – Time: 15 minutes
Using Sheet 7 on page 78 record some of your talk from yesterday. Start from when you woke up, and retrace your footsteps as if you are replaying a video of your life. In order to take a more analytical look at talk, consider who, why and how you were talking. Do you notice any

patterns? Is there any type of talk which particularly dominates? If you recorded your talk for another day of the week how might it be different?

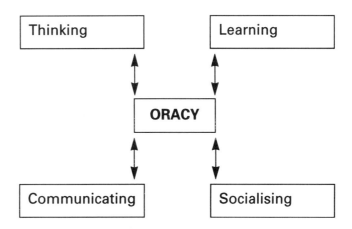

Figure 4.1 Oracy as a transmitter for processes

Why is talk useful?

Once we start to examine talk more closely we can begin to see that it is useful in many different ways. When working in educational settings it is important to have a good awareness and understanding of these diverse functions of talk. With this knowledge we can ensure that the learners are using talk to its fullest potential. Figure 4.2 below illustrates the major functions of talk.

WHY IS TALK USEFUL?

- Talk communicates meaning
- Talk communicates feelings
- Talk communicates intention
- Talk conveys instructions
- Talk conveys responses — to people and experiences
- Talk can recall the past
- Talk can predict the future
- Talk reshapes and reinforces understanding
- We answer questions through talk
- We ask questions through talk
- Talk allows the exploration and development of ideas by externalising thought

Figure 4.2 The major functions of talk

What does the National Curriculum say about oracy?

When the National Curriculum for English was first presented in 1989, many teachers were pleased to see that a whole attainment target was dedicated to speaking and listening. This recognition of the place of oracy in children's learning reflected how important the spoken word is within the language opportunities which should be provided for young children.

The revised Order for English, introduced in 1995, still includes speaking and listening as a discrete attainment target. It is also important to note that the reading and writing sections refer to talk as a vital part of children's language work. Likewise, in other areas of the curriculum talk is identified as a required mode of working.

Making and playing with puppets provides an excellent context for talk.

'Pupils should be encouraged to talk for different purposes with a range of people, learning to vary what they say and how they say it, according to the context. The Key Skills section specifies the development of pupils' participation in discussion and attentive listening. Pupils' knowledge and use of Standard English is to be developed in the context of their understanding of variety in language. Also included here are requirements for active involvement in drama and critical engagement with media'. (SCAA, TTA and ACAC, 1996 – page 18).

Different types of talk

As you will have discovered from Activity 1, there are many different types of talk. When working with early years children a good professional knowledge of the range of talk possible helps us to stimulate, support and extend children in the development of their speaking and listening skills.

The following types of talk are referred to specifically in the National Curriculum Programmes of Study for English, A.T.1.

- Key stage 1
  telling stories
  reading aloud
  exploring
  developing ideas
  clarifying ideas

predicting
discussing
describing
explaining
justifying (opinions and actions)
comments on talk by others
role play

● You should also consider the following:
questioning
decision making
expanding
evaluating
instructing

ACTIVITY 4.2 — Time: 20 minutes if writing from memory OR 30 minutes actual observation in your workplace
Make a chart on which to record the different types of talk you have observed in your early years workplace. Use columns to define different curriculum areas of learning, or alternatively the different activitiy areas available to the children. In each column record the types of talk (e.g. questioning, explaining), and the social context (e.g. group of four, individual). Are there any relationships between certain types of talk and certain activities or curriculum areas? Does any type of talk dominate?

Extending children's spontaneous talk

Every interaction in a nursery or early years classroom is an opportunity for developing children's talk. However, we cannot assume that just because talk is happening that learning is taking place. On the contrary, there are many occasions where the talk might be off-task and the interactions unproductive. So how can those who support the work of teachers ensure that their input is making a valuable contribution towards extending children's learning and developing their oracy skills?

The reasons for adult intervention fall into five main types — initiation, information, feedback, prevention and response. It is useful for those working with children to develop an awareness of how they are using these types of intervention.

ACTIVITY 4.3 — Time: ongoing
This activity is designed to enable you to reflect upon your own interactions with the children in your workplace. Make a copy of Sheet 8 on page 79 and place it on a clipboard or hard-file for easy reference. Take one or two questions as a focus each day and record any thoughts on the sheet. The bottom of the sheet includes an 'Action Points' section for you to identify any changes which you may wish to make as a result of your observations.

Promoting good listening skills

Some adults find it hard to listen; sometimes they hear without listening. Children are just the same. The mistake is often made of assuming that

23

because children are sitting still and quietly on the classroom carpet that they are listening well.

PAUSE FOR THOUGHT: How do you find out if a child has been listening?

With skilled questioning and checking back one can usually tune in to the level of listening which has taken place. However when a child cannot answer your questions, it is important to consider whether it is because they have not listened or because they have not understood. In actual fact they might have been daydreaming. This 'trancing out' or switching off from the events around us is a highly developed safety mechanism which can sometimes be extremely useful when our brains are tired or in danger of being overloaded. However, it can also be a distracting habit which prevents children from listening and learning — a barrier to communication.

In order to help us understand why children tune out from listening let us consider all the reasons why we, as adults do the same thing. It might be because we are:

bored
nervous
feeling outstripped by more vociferous group members
feeling unable to express what we feel
fearful of criticism
fearful of saying the wrong thing

PAUSE FOR THOUGHT: Can you think of any other reasons why you may become detached from a group situation? Taking the examples above plus any additional ones of your own can you match these to particular situations in which you have found yourself recently?

Planning for talk

Those who support the work of teachers in early years settings are not always directly responsible for the planning of activities, but many are included in team preparations. It is probably helpful, therefore, for you to know some of the main principles which can lie behind the planning of talk activities in order to help you contribute fully to any such team discussions. It is hoped that this will also help you to understand the reasoning behind teachers' thinking. In this way you will develop a more informed awareness of the purpose of planned talk and in turn make an even more valuable contribution in your role as supporting adult to pupils and teachers.

Figure 4.3 below illustrates eight important aspects which should be considered when planning talk activities.

1. Curriculum area. Talk happens right across the curriculum range and opportunities for developing different types of talk can be identified in a clear and purposeful way.
EXAMPLE: Water tray → science → explaining

2. Purpose of the activity. Children are far more likely to become involved in an activity if it has a clear and meaningful purpose.
EXAMPLE: Cooking → technology → each child takes turns to give instructions to the next child

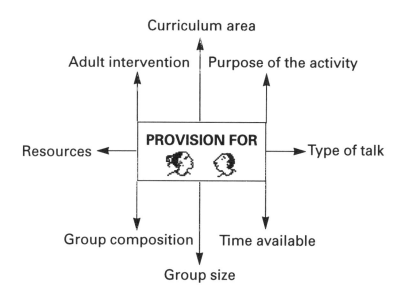

Figure 4.3 Things to consider when planning talk activities

3. Type of talk. If children are to develop a range of skills for communication through talking, it is important to monitor which types of talk they have had opportunities to practise.

EXAMPLE: Group of children showing models to the rest of the children ⟶ technology⟶asking the model-makers questions about their experiences

4. Time to be allocated. As with all activities, children will wander off-task very quickly if they are bored, struggling, or have finished. However, children will always continue to talk. It is important, therefore, that the purpose and necessity for the talk is monitored time-wise.

EXAMPLE: Show-and-tell ⟶ 5 minutes for child to tell, 5 minutes for questions, 5 minutes reporting back on how much they can remember.

5. Group size. This can vary according to the activity, but can certainly make a difference to the quality of input. Pairs work well, a trio can involve an observer/recorder dynamic, fours tend to need more rules. Large group discussions need very clear ground rules and these are best established in consultation with the children themselves. Too long in a large group situation can become frustrating for many children, hence the 'restlessness on the carpet' syndrome.

EXAMPLE: Story-making⟶make up a story in pairs⟶split up and go and tell a new partner your story.

6. Group composition. Self-selected friendship groups are sometimes appropriate, but sometimes it is valuable to place children with certain others for example it is sometimes appropriate to group all the vociferous children together, not just to give the others more of a chance, but also to help the vocal children to practise their listening and social skill. Be aware of the effects which group composition has upon the quality of the talk.

EXAMPLES OF COMBINATIONS: ability, mixed ability, boys, girls, talkative, shy.

7. Resources. Merely being asked to talk is rarely enough to keep any group on task for a sufficiently useful time. Talk tends to have a life of its own. This can be exciting and creative, but sometimes it can also mean that children are wandering off the learning track into distracting and less productive interactions. Careful consideration of resources can enhance the quality of talk considerably and also help children to stay on-task. Resources are also an important means of ensuring that the children have something to talk about!

Resources can be divided broadly into three categories:

1. stimulus resources
2. support resources
3. recording resources

Stimulus resources are those which help get the talk started. For instance pictures, artefacts, stories, visitors. It is difficult for children to learn how to use the powers of description if they are not given interesting objects and experiences to describe.

Support resources are resources which provide the talk with some form of frame-work. Examples might include a shell to hold when taking turns to talk, instructions to follow and prompt cards.

Recording resources can be a way of providing a goal or end-product for the talk. Examples of this might include large sheets of paper and felt-tips for brainstorming (in pictures or words as appropriate), lists of things needed to make a model after discussing first, Children need cues and support for their talk,

EXAMPLE: Measuring distance of toy cars down a ramp→maths→discuss and record the distances in order by drawing them on a prepared sheet.

8. Adult intervention. Interventions can be made in many ways including listening, questioning, instructing, reminding, to name but a few. Planned intervention can help to ensure that the talk stays on task, rather than waiting until a hub-bub arises to attract you over to the activity.

EXAMPLE: Describing their houses→geography→say that you are not going to join in for the first five minutes, but watch to see how well they are listening to each other. Then ask questions and direct the next part of the task.

Managing talk

You will all recognise children you have worked with who are often reluctant to talk, or who rarely take a turn in large groups. Certain management techniques can help you plan to overcome this. One such technique is sometimes called 'rainbowing', where children working in groups are each given a colour. They then move into a new group, along with children who have the same colour, where they have to report back. Reporting back, or explaining/describing to a partner can also be a good way to encourage quieter children.

ACTIVITY 4.4 — Time: 30 minutes
Imagine that you are assigned to work with a group on 'Homes and Houses'. The teacher wants the children to make decisions about a range of options for house design. Make a resource which you think will help to keep the children on-task and which will influence this type of decision-making talk.

The resources, challenges and goals provided by adults can motivate the right sorts of talk, and are therefore also useful management mechanisms. In other words, if children are going to engage in a range of talk activities they need appropriate purposes for their talk supported by relevant resources as discussed in more detail previously in this chapter.

Last but not least, talking about talk helps children to understand the significance of what they are doing. There is much value in drawing attention to the types of talk as they are being used and discussing the qualities which are required in different situations. Praising children for the ways in which they are speaking is just as appropriate as praising them for their reading and writing. Likewise with listening. If you make it clear to children that you value their turn-taking behaviour, for example, they are more likely to demonstrate this on future occasions. Perhaps most importantly, the children will grow to recognise the importance and power of their own oracy.

Notes for group leaders	⇨	Discuss Activity 4.1 with the whole group.

⇨ Discuss Activity 4.2 in pairs.

⇨ Use partners to give feedback and constructive suggestions after Activity 4.3.

⇨ Look at the National Curriculum Order for English and discuss the references to Standard English in Attainment Target 1. (Whole group.)

⇨ Discuss when it is not appropriate to intervene in children's talk. (Whole group.)

⇨ Discuss the issues around 'correcting' children's speech. (Whole group.)

⇨ In groups of three, brainstorm ideas on how you might encourage certain types of talk in the following situations: water play, maths, art.

Further reading

Edwards,V. (1995). *Speaking and Listening in Multilingual Classrooms*. Reading: Reading and Language Information Centre.

Fidge, L. (1992). *The Essential Guide to Speaking and Listening*. Dunstable: Folens.

Norman, K. (1990). *Teaching, Talking and Learning in Key Stage 1*. York: National Curriculum Council.

SCCA, TTA and ACAC (1996) *A Guide to the National Curriculum*. London: SCAA Publications, p. 18.

CHAPTER 5

The complexity of reading

Reading is a complex process and yet, as adult readers, we tend to take this process for granted. If we are to support children when they are learning to read, it is important for us to understand how they feel, and to remind ourselves of the strategies which are needed when a reader is faced with text that is new and challenging. This chapter explores the process of reading in order to help you understand what children are experiencing as developing readers, the strategies they need to learn and how you can support them effectively.

The importance of reading

Whenever standards in schools are under scrutiny, reading is usually at the centre of the debate. When parents express concern to teachers about their child's progress it is more often than not about his or her reading. When the government expresses concern about levels of pupils' performance it usually includes their performance in reading. It is easy to see why reading has such an important place in our society — not only is it central to learning across the curriculum, it is also an important skill which is required every day by the majority of people.

The importance of reading.

Supermarkets are packed with print.

Symbols are also contributing to children's concepts of print.

ACTIVITY 5.1— Time: 10 minutes

Think about some of the places you have visited during the past few days. This might include work, college, shops, bus station, train station, watching TV or the doctor's waiting room. On a blank sheet of paper, jot down all the examples of text which you can remember from those situations.

When we stop to think of this tremendous range of texts which we read automatically it becomes apparent just how significant reading is in our lives. There are the texts which we actively seek out to read for the purposes of our work, our leisure and to perform many important operations within the running of our life. Then there are the texts which confront us continuously in and around the environment.

Do we read everything in the same way?

Having identified examples of the texts which you encounter every day, let us now consider how you approach those texts. Imagine all the mail which might be delivered through your door on a typical day. The first envelope is your telephone bill. You know this before you have even opened it because of the type, colour and size of print, and also the recognisable logo — you have already used reading skills to make sense of this visual information. What do you do when you have unfolded the papers inside the envelope? Do you start at the top left-hand corner and read systematically from left to right down the page until you have finished? Almost certainly, the answer to this question will be 'no'! It is much more likely that you scan straight down to the total to see how much you owe. Consider how people read a menu. Some may look at the wine list on the back page first so that they can enjoy a drink while choosing the meal. Others may look at the puddings first, or some may be looking just at the prices to spot the best bargain. A train timetable involves quite complex cross-referencing whereas a set of self-assembly instructions needs to be read systematically in sequential order. If you are reading a non-fiction book you are quite likely to refer to the contents page and also the index, whereas you are unlikely to read down the list of chapter titles of a romantic novel, unless, of course, you want some clues about the story in advance! In other words, we use different reading skills for different purposes.

ACTIVITY 5.2 - TIME: 20 minutes

Using Sheet 9, think carefully about the different types of texts listed. Then, taking each one at a time, try to recall exactly what you do when you read. This might include such things as where you start, how much detail, how much you need to understand, the parts you ignore and the order you read.

By focusing on all these different ways in which you read you will start to develop an awareness of just how complicated the reading process is. Early years children are engaged in developing a wide range of skills, knowledge and understanding about reading to enable them to take part effectively in this process. If you are to support them in a way which encourages this development, it is important for you to understand what is actually taking place when readers read.

What do we do when we read?

When you started to read this chapter how did you look at the text? Did you look at the individual letters and build up the sounds, taking each word separately to construct the sentences? Probably not. It is more likely that you recognised whole words and moved along the lines of writing in chunks. Speed readers are even able to read down the page taking in whole lines of text at once.

Experienced readers rarely need to 'sound out' the letters to build up a word as early readers do. They have developed the ability to see and identify whole words as single units — word recognition skills. However, if they encounter a strange word which they have not seen before they will probably need to go back to building up the letters into sounds, whilst at the same time drawing upon their knowledge of letter patterns from more familiar words which are similar in order to help with pronunciation and emphasis.

In order to try and experience how that works, here is a simple task. Look at the word below and try to say it out loud.

KNEBEVIGHT

You probably said something which sounded like 'neebvite'. Why did you not pronounce the K, the second E, and the G and H? You already know words with these silent letters and patterns in them and so you transferred the rules across. In other words you used your knowledge of letter shapes, letter sounds and spelling rules to say the word.

So you have read the word aloud, but have you really read it? No! All you have done is translated shapes into sounds. At the moment there is no meaning. Let us look at the word again in a sentence.

SALLY PULLED HER KNEBEVIGHT

How many possible meanings can you think of for this strange word? We know now that the word is a noun because of its relationship with the other words in the sentence. But is this in fact a sentence? Where is the full-stop? Let's have some more clues.

SALLY PULLED HER KNEBEVIGHT ON

The addition of one more word makes an enormous difference to our understanding of the word, and yet still there is no clear meaning. Nor is there yet a full stop.

SALLY PULLED HER KNEBEVIGHT ON TO KEEP HERSELF WARM.

That narrows it down a bit, and yet even so the word could still have a variety of meanings — coat, hat, duvet. . . . We have arrived at the end of the sentence because now we have a full-stop. However, we still need more information in order to understand the meaning of our mystery word. If there was a picture we might be able to see what Sally was pulling on. In the absence of a picture, let us look further on in the text.

SHE WRAPPED IT AROUND HER NECK SEVERAL TIMES

Is there an outside chance that the knebevight could be a pet python? Read on!

. . . AND ALTHOUGH THE COLOURS OF HER FAVOURITE FOOTBALL TEAM CLASHED VIOLENTLY WITH HER HAT, SHE WAS TRULY GRATEFUL FOR ITS PROTECTION FROM THE BITING WIND.

I think we can be pretty sure now that the knebevight is a scarf!

In order to read those two sentences for meaning the following strategies had to be used:

● sound out the letters
● build up letter patterns
● apply knowledge of other words and rules
● connect the relationship of the words grammatically
● use the context for clues

For the purposes of this very simple exercise these strategies took place one at a time because the text was unfolded to you in parts. However, under normal reading conditions the effective reader employs all those strategies almost simultaneously when encountering new words. An early reader, however, has not yet developed the skills to employ this range of strategies in such a sophisticated way. Learning to do this requires teaching, practice and experience of a range of texts and strategies.

ACTIVITY 5.3 — Time: 15 minutes

Find or make a copy of Sheet 8 *but cover it up immediately* with a sheet of paper! Read the instructions at the top then uncover one piece of text at a time to analyse what strategies you have to use to decipher these rather unusual texts.

By now, you will have developed an awareness of the fact that when we read we employ different sorts of strategies in order to make sense of the text. Let us now look at how these strategies differ from each other as this can help deepen our understanding of the reading process even further.

Engagements with the text

The strategies which we use when we read can be divided into four categories. which are illustrated below in Figure 5.1.

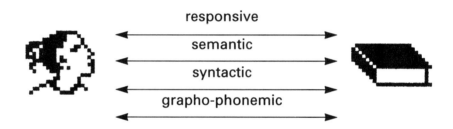

Figure 5.1 The four categories of engagement

The diagram represents the reader, the text and the four types of relating which take place between the two. These are called **categories of engagement** because they are pathways which 'engage' or 'connect' the reader in some way with the text.

1. Responsive engagement

This type of engagement is where the reader is responding to what they have read. At the very early levels of reading this might include a toddler pointing to a picture and laughing. At a more developed stage this could mean a child talking about why they do not like a certain character and predicting what is going to happen next. Response is more than understanding because it brings to the text the reader's own experiences and individuality.

2. Semantic engagement

Semantic engagement is the level at which the reader is making meaning from the text. It is about understanding what has been read.

3. Syntactic engagement

The syntax of the text is the organisation and structure. Written English is built with specific systems which have rules. Understanding these conventions helps the child to decipher and understand the text. For example, full stops give us important information to help us make sense of what we read.

4. Grapho-phonemic engagement

The 'graph' part means visual and the 'phon' part means sound. Quite simply, this aspect of reading is about seeing the shapes of the letters and transforming them into the sounds which make words. It is often referred to as 'decoding' the text.

ACTIVITY 5.4 — Time: 10 minutes
Refer back to the notes you made during Activity 5.3 and try to allocate each of the strategies you used to one of the four categories.

By going through this process you will notice that there is overlap and inter-weaving between the categories of engagement. It is most important to remember that they work alongside each other when the reader is experienced. However, when children are in the early stages of learning to read, they will use strategies in isolation. For example, a child may read in 'robot-voice' a page from their book without any errors and yet when they reach the end they are unable to recall what they have read.

There are several important things to remember about the four categories of engagement.

- They are not learned in a special order one after the other.
- Individual readers will use them in different proportions.
- Some children need support within one category more than others.
- The effective reader uses them in combination.

Having a theoretical framework in mind is only useful if we can relate it to what is actually happening in practice. Let us now turn to the early years settings in which children are learning to read so that we can identify where this knowledge can be applied usefully. In order to do this, we must have a clear understanding of the commonly-used ways of referring to the developmental stages of reading, some of which have been used already in this chapter.

Developmental progress of reading in the early years

Some years ago, early years teachers were trained to teach what were called 'pre-reading' or 'reading readiness' skills. These included activities such as matching, listening, sight recognition and memory games and were provided in order to 'prepare' children for reading. In extreme cases, the child would only be given a reading book once they knew enough letters and sound to be able to decode that book.

Today, such games continue to be a useful part of children's learning, but the notion that this is preparing them for a special point in their development at which they can be recognised as a reader has changed. This is because children are already considered to be well on their way to reading (and writing) before they start to decode text. This is known as 'emergent literacy'.

The 'emergent reader' is the child who knows what books are for, who enjoys stories, can talk about books, and is already aware of the function of print. It is staggering how much children already know about reading by the time they start nursery or playgroup. The word 'TESCO' on a carrier bag, the 'STOP' sign at the end of the road, the shopping list, the birthday card - they all carry particular messages which are understood by many young children. Earlier in this chapter you stopped to focus on the variety of print in your life. Such a stimulating print environment has a profound effect on the early learning of young children and it should not be ignored because it provides a healthy foundation on which learning can grow. Therefore, the development of the reader should be thought of in terms of a continual line rather than a series of steps.

As the child begins to learn more systematically about the components of reading, the letters, sounds, words and grammar. He or she begins to move towards becoming a 'supported reader'. At this stage the child is showing an interest in tackling some print with the help of a more experienced reader. He or she will look at books for pleasure but needs help to tackle unfamiliar texts.

Gradually the child develops into a 'fluent reader' as he or she builds up her knowledge of how texts work. The child will tend to revisit familiar texts which he or she will read with confidence, but also approach new texts with increasing skill. At this stage, the child will start to read some parts of some texts silently.

Eventually, it is hoped that the child will develop into an 'independent reader'. Typically, a child at this stage will be choosing texts from a range of sources, will understand what is read and be able to discuss it with reference to the text. The child will also be starting to read between the lines for hidden meanings.

Reading and writing are closely interlinked.

Which model of reading is required by the National Curriculum?

The Order for English requires a programme of study which enables children to read a wide range of texts for different purposes. This includes poetry, prose, plays, non-fiction, media and IT-based texts. Literature should be by a representative selection of authors and from a range of genres, including stories from different cultures and traditions. The Order recognises that children should be taught by a range of methods, and that an integrated approach which incorporates writing and oracy is desirable.

'This wide reading experience will enable pupils to develop strategies for reading, and in locating and using information. They should also be encouraged to read responsively and critically.' (SCAA, TTA and ACAC, 1996).

How should reading be taught?

Over the years there have been many 'fashionable' ways of teaching reading. These so-called methods have tended to spring from research into the different strategies used by the reader. For example:

The Phonic Method relied on learning letters and sounds even before reading books were issued to children.

Traditional Reading Schemes *(e.g. Janet and John)* provided repetitive reinforcing texts which introduced new words progressively within graded books.

The Look and Say Method was based on the theory that readers read whole word shapes and should therefore learn single words out of context.

The Initial Teaching Alphabet (ita) method involved a whole new system of letters and rules which allowed children to read words which were spelt as they sounded.

The Language and Experience Method used much of children's own talking and writing experiences as resources for reading.

The Apprenticeship Approach highlighted the importance of using a wide variety of quality literature which is meaningful and enjoyable to the child along with adult support. Booktalk between child and adult was identified as a significant factor in children's reading development.

New Reading Schemes *(e.g. The Oxford Reading Tree)* are now an indication that publishers have listened to the disparaging comparisons between old scheme and 'real' literature. New schemes now tend to include a range of text types (fiction, non-fiction, poetry, plays) by different authors. The quality of the stories and illustrations have been improved considerably.

Having been subject to this swinging pendulum of educational trends, teachers are now recognising that extreme methods which focus on one particular strategy are not appropriate in themselves if children are to learn the wide range of skills required for effective reading. It is widely agreed that a range of methods should be employed in order to develop the number of required strategies, and that some children will need more of some than others. Also, the integration of reading with writing and oracy experiences enhances and enriches children's learning and helps them to develop appropriate skills in meaningful contexts. Above all, children should be developing positive perceptions of themselves as readers so that they actively seek to interrogate, explore and enjoy texts of all kinds.

Notes for group leaders

⇨ In pairs, sort the examples from Activity 5.2 into 'types' of reading.

⇨ Activity 5.3 could be conducted with the whole group by making an overhead projector copy of Sheet 8.

⇨ Discussions about the nature of support will be useful as will opportunities to experience and feed back on giving support to other group members. Photocopy a piece of text (if possible with pictures) onto an overhead projector skin then turn the skin the wrong way and make paper copies so that the text is back-to-front. Get the group to work in pairs, one taking the role of supporting adult helping the other who is the reader. After five minutes of 'reading' ask them to reflect on the strategies they were using to decipher and understand the text and what was helpful from their partner. Discuss as a large group.

⇨ In groups of three, make a collection of examples of print which are not on paper and make a display.

⇨ In groups of four, brainstorm ideas for linking reading and writing in a nursery class.

Further reading

Beard, R. (1987). *Developing Reading 3–13*. London: Hodder & Stoughton

Clarke, M. (1994). *Young Literacy Learners — How We Can Help Them*. Leamington Spa: Scholastic

Clay, M. (1991). *Becoming Literate*. Auckland: Heinemann.

Roberts, G. (1994). *Learning to Teach Reading*. Hemel Hempstead: Simon & Schuster Education.

SCAA, TTA and ACAC (1996) *A Guide to the National Curriculum*. London: SCAA Publications.

University of Derby (1994). *The Teaching of Reading*. Derby: University of Derby.

CHAPTER 6

Supporting children's reading activities

The previous chapter aimed to increase your understanding of the reading process in order to inform your working practices. This chapter attempts to link that theoretical knowledge to the everyday actualities of working with children. It examines the relationship skills which can contribute to the quality of support offered by adults to children when they are engaged in reading activities. The nature of this support is then discussed within the context of different reading activities commonly found in nurseries and early years classrooms.

The reading relationship

Those who assist in early years settings spend much of their time supporting children's reading across a wide range of activities. These include working individually with one child, working with different sized groups and sometimes reading stories to the whole class. The quality of the relationship between child and supporting adult can have a significant effect on the productivity of those activities. Not only does it influence the development of the child's reading it can also affect how the child perceives herself as a reader.

To begin, let us focus on what we mean by 'support'. Figure 6.1 below illustrates four main components of support for children's reading.

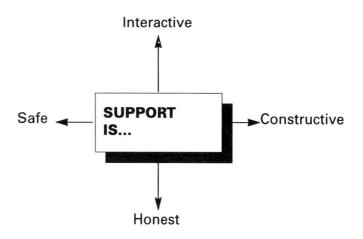

Figure 6.1 Components of support

These four components encompass all the important qualities required to support children with their reading. Let us look at each in turn.

1. Support is interactive

To be a passive onlooker is to miss opportunities for helping the child. You are a valuable resource for learning. However, advice, guidance and information can be offered in many different ways and it is important that you do not regard yourself as a 'knowledge machine'. The support needs to be a two-way process so that you and the child are responding to each other. The following points should be considered:

- How can I find out what the child needs to know?
- How can the child be encouraged to ask questions?
- How can the child learn from my example?
- How does the child perceive my explanations?
- How can I check that the child understands what has been discussed?
- How can I be a good reading role model?
- Do I leave enough space for the child to respond?

2. Support is constructive

A constructive approach to learning means building on what is already there in a positive and developmental way. When a child shares their ideas and expertise with an adult they are placing great trust in that adult. For some children that can be quite nerve-wracking because they feel they are laying themselves open to criticism. If we start from a sound base of the child's current expertise we can always find a positive focus. Children respond more effectively to praise than criticism, and building on their expertise has the additional benefit of developing their self-esteem.

- Do I always pounce immediately on the mistakes?
- If so, what impact does this have on the child?
- Am I aware of individual differences between children's abilities and needs?
- How can I identify what the child is already doing well?
- How can I praise sincerely?
- How can I offer constructive feedback?
- Do I give children the opportunity to revisit and practice the areas of feedback?

3. Support is honest

Honesty is important in any relationship. Children soon know if an adult is patronising them or giving praise where praise is not due. Being honest in the reading relationship is not necessarily about pointing out all the mistakes, but it can be about the following:

- Talking about the books you read at home.
- Giving your own opinions about the book you are sharing.
- Disagreeing with the child in an OK way!
- Allowing the child to disagree with you in an OK way!
- Giving positive feedback before identifying areas for development.

- Asking the child for their opinions.
- Encouraging children to be honest with each other.

4. Support is safe

If children are to try their very best and are determined to succeed they have to take risks. If they are afraid to try an unknown word because they are afraid of getting it wrong their learning will be held back. However, if they trust the adults with whom they work they will be more likely to experiment and explore within their own learning, and in this way they will be constantly pushing out the boundaries of their learning experience. Examples of this might include the books they choose, the ideas they express, disagreeing with your opinions about books, asking questions, making decisions about their own learning and so on.

- How do I show children that I respect their expertise?
- Do I encourage children to take risks (e.g. have a go at a strange word)?
- Do I ensure that children are comfortable?
- Do I give children the time they need?
- Do I provide opportunities for children to explore their own learning?
- How do I show children that I value their efforts?

ACTIVITY 6.1—Time: 15 minutes
Reflect on the support which you give to the children in your care in three situations—with individuals, small groups and the whole class (if appropriate). On a sheet of paper write down what you consider to be your strengths in each situation and then identify the areas which you would like to change, improve or develop. If it is possible, try to discuss these notes with an adult who can support you in making these changes.

Listening to children read

This is a task which predominates the work of many supporting assistants and parent helpers in infant classes. There is sometimes a danger that this can become a regimented chore when a list has to be completed, and the children have to be 'got through' like numbered cattle. Therefore, let us stop to consider that for the child this is an important time and a time which deserves quality input from you. It is worth remembering that each child will bring to this experience a different agenda. Here are some examples:

> "Oh, good! It's my turn!"
> "Oh, no! It's my turn!"
> "Why does she always call me when I'm doing something good?"
> "I hope I can read properly today."
> "Why does it always have to be me?"

You can probably think of many more. The agenda will be influenced, to a large extent, by the way the child has experienced this time with you previously. In other words if you were cross with the child for mispronouncing words yesterday he or she is unlikely to feel very enthusiastic about repeating the process today.

There are three questions which you need to consider when hearing children read. How can you ensure that the experience is enjoyable for the child? How can you ensure that the experience is a valuable learning time for the child? How can you feed back information which will be useful to the teacher?

The following suggestions are provided to give you some guidelines which apply equally to situations where you might be reading to a child who has not yet started to decode text.

Ensuring that the experience is enjoyable for the child

Putting children at their ease is not merely about being a kind person. It is about creating an atmosphere in which children want to learn and feel motivated to work to their optimum ability.

- Be sensitive in your timing.
- Try to invite the child to share a book with you rather than summoning him or her.
- Put the child at ease by asking them how he or she.
- Ask them about the book they have chosen to read before asking them to read it.
- Do not rush the child — leave time for self-correction.
- Respond to what the child is doing well and be encouraging.

Ensuring that the experience is a valuable learning time for the child

Part of the skill of extending children's learning is to select appropriately. Obviously if you attempted to do all the things listed below the poor child would hardly find time to read! Consider carefully, in consultation with the teacher, what the child can already do in order to identify which of the interventions below are appropriate. Interrupting the flow can be unproductive if it is frustrating the child's efforts and distracting their concentration.

- Let the child hold the book and turn the pages, even if you are doing the reading.
- Talk together about the book features (cover, front, back and author etc.).
- Talk together about the pictures.
- Talk together about the characters.
- Talk together about the language features (letters, words, spaces etc.).
- Talk together about experiences relating to the story (e.g. the child's pet).
- Encourage the child to look for clues when reading.
- Encourage the child to build up the sounds of words.
- Encourage the child to read for meaning in small chunks
- Allow time to revisit or practice areas of uncertainty.
- Read along with the child if they need support.
- Where you are doing all the reading, encourage the child to predict or guess some of the words as you read.
- Encourage the child to predict and explain.

Giving useful feedback to the teacher

If you have spent a period of quality learning time with any one child you are bound to have collected vital information which could prove useful to the teacher. Nurseries and schools vary in the ways in which reading time is recorded, but try to consider the following points when feeding back information.

- Make your comments informative. 'Jason read well' tells me nothing. Does this mean that Jason read fluently, understood what he read, read with expression or read new words? A comment such as 'Jason is starting to read ahead in the sentence to find contextual clues.' is far more useful.
- The mistakes which children make when they are reading can be extremely useful. Try to note these down if there is an obvious pattern. For example, 'Seems to have a problem with -ing endings.'
- Take note of the child's attitude towards reading and books.

ACTIVITY 6.2 — Time: 40 minutes
Please check with the teacher before doing this activity. Make a copy of Sheet 9 and arrange to share a book with the child that you and the teacher have chosen. Try to make this the same as your normal practice so that the child feels comfortable. You will probably need to do most of the recording afterwards, although it writing in reading record books is part of the normal practice then it should be all right to jot notes down during the activity. It is probably wise to do this exercise with a range of children so that one child does not feel he or she has been singled out. It will certainly be useful for you to compare different children.

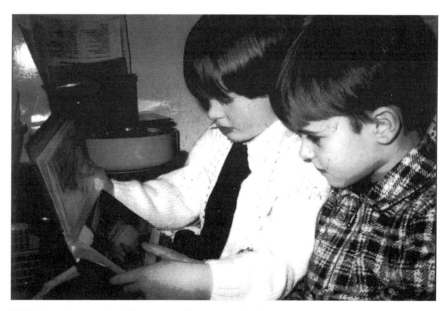

Children love looking at photos and these can be used to make interesting books.

Paired reading

The term 'paired reading' was coined in the 1970s and refers to a specific type of reading partnership. It is a partnership in which the child reads to the adult, the adult reads to the child and sometimes the two read simultaneously. The important feature is that the child is in control of this and can decide who reads and when. This is usually signalled by nudging elbows or patting on the hand. Putting the child in the driving seat like this can be extremely reassuring to children who lack confidence with their reading. The adult is there to support as and when the child needs them.

Shared reading

Shared reading is the term applied to two people enjoying a book together. This might mean two children of the same age, an older child and a younger child or a child and an adult. The reading can be shared as decided by the children, but the central feature of shared reading is the booktalk which also takes place during this time. Talking about books plays an important role in the development of readers. Discussing the pictures, the characters, the action, the author's style, predicting, explaining, questioning, empathising, comparing and so on all enrich children's understanding of and responses to books.

Children benefit from talking about what they are reading.

Group reading

In recent years group reading has enjoyed a revival. It is particularly effective for older children who are starting to read independently, but benefit from the supported framework provided by reading in a group. Each child has a copy of one text and they take turns reading aloud while the rest of the group follow the text in their own copy. The practice is often extended into follow-up activities which provide the children with opportunities to explore particular aspects of language using the story or play as a starting point.

Reading games

Reading games are not only an enjoyable activity for children, they are also a valuable resource for learning. The many skills of reading can be placed within the context of a game to provide an opportunity to repeat, revisit and practise in ways which are motivating and meaningful.

There are many types of games which are commercially available, but it is also possible to make games. Classroom assistants on the Specialist Teacher's Assistant Course at Oxford Brookes University School of Education were asked to make a reading game using early years fiction as a starting point and theme. The design, making and evaluation of the game constituted one of the assignments for their course. The ideas they came up with were absolutely superb. They included game boards (*Rosie's Walk* by Pat Hutchins), cloze procedure (*Going on a Bear Hunt* by Michael Rosen), matching (*Dear Zoo* by Rod Cambell), sorting, rhyming snap (*Each Peach Pear Plum* by J. and A. Ahlberg), sentence making (*The Snowman* by Raymond Briggs) and many more.

Trialling the games with groups of children was also an exciting part of their work. The enjoyment and learning was very evident, but they were also able to make adjustments to their games based on observations of how they worked in practice. Needless to say the teacher mentors were delighted with these additional resources for their classrooms, and the next phase of the project will be to encourage the assistants to lead groups of volunteer parents in the making of games for different classrooms according to the needs specified by the teachers.

Using stories as starting points for games has many benefits. The game can be planned to introduce and use specific skills, but in addition there are golden opportunities for talking about the book, characters, plot, author and so on. Games relating to specific books encourage children to use the language of those books and contribute to the literary environment.

ACTIVITY 6.3 — Time: 6 hours
Part 1 — Making a Reading Game
Using children's literature as a starting point for activities in the classroom is just one way of enriching the literary environment in schools. Bearing this in mind, your are invited to make a reading game which is based upon a picture book. It can take any form you wish - e.g. board game, card game, tape, etc. Think carefully about which specific aspects of reading the game addresses. Try to imagine the processes which a child will go through as he or she plays the game. These may not be the same as adult processes. It would be wise to include an instruction card in the game so that other adults will understand how to use it.

Try to ensure that any texts and pictures within the game are clear and professional. You may wish to use word processing for this rather than handwritten print. If you are able to laminate the game it is likely to last considerably longer than if it is used in its unprotected form.

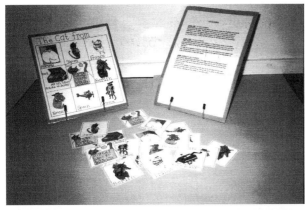

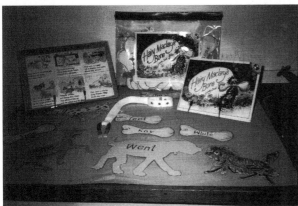

These reading games, using picture books as starting points, were made by STA course students at Oxford Brookes University.

Part 2—A Written Analysis of Your Game
This is *not* an explanation of how to play the game, but a justification of the methods employed. How is the game going to support the children who plays it? What skills is it helping to develop? You may wish to support your explanations with references to background reading, but this is not essential. Ideally, you will be able to show this to your teacher or group leader in order to receive some feedback. If this is not possible, it is nevertheless a useful process to evaluate your work for yourself. Perhaps you could exchange feedback with a fellow assistant who would also like to try this activity. The following questions might help you to do this:

> Does the game clearly address specific reading skills?
> Have I demonstrated a good understanding of those skills?
> Are the playing instructions clear?
> Is the game well made and attractively presented?
> Have I reflected on my observations of children playing the game?
> Can I adjust the game according to those observations?

Reading across the curriculum

Many of the reading development activities which take place in early years settings are discrete. In other words, they are specifically about language and literacy. However, there are also opportunities for reading to be developed in other subject areas. Here are some examples in order to develop your thinking about how you can extend children's reading skills in all areas of the curriculum.

Maths	matching shapes
	sorting and counting letters
Science	labels on displays
	talk about photographs
History	look at old books
	use of non-fiction books
Geography	directionality
	catalogues of home furnishings
Art	directionality
	shape and letter patterns
Technology	pop-up books
	puppets
Movement	characters from books
	journeys and explorations from books
Music	rhythm and rhyme
	sounds and listening games
IT	reading game instructions
	word processing
Media	newspapers and magazines
	television texts
RE	religious books and stories
	stories from other cultures

Clearly, it will be the teacher's responsibility to plan for these areas. However, it is important to remember that informed support for reading across the curriculum can make a real contribution to the continued development of children's reading. The discussion, explaining, comparing, repeating and matching which might take place with a story book are just as valid and as fruitful with non-fiction texts. It is also worth remembering to read aloud extracts from non-fiction for discussion as well as fiction.

ACTIVITY 6.4 — Time: 30 minutes
If you have never worked in a nursery, it might be a good idea to arrange a visit before attempting this next activity. Using Sheet 10 think carefully about all the different types of activities listed and make notes about your ideas for developing certain aspects of reading during those activities. These might relate to an interest in books, awareness of print, recognition of letters or words for instance. How might you extend the interventions you make with children in order to capitalise on every opportunity for learning?

Environmental print

The prominence and importance of print have already been discussed in the previous chapter. Let us now consider how this can be used to the children's advantage in an educational setting.

It is very easy to collect a whole range of cost-free materials from all kinds of establishments. For example

- Shops
- Garages
- Transport depot
- Tourist information centres

- Hotels
- Restaurants
- Used magazines and newspapers

can be a rich source of

- Leaflets
- Brochures
- Catalogues
- Posters
- Display materials
- Window dressing materials
- Advertisements
- Boxes

- Scrap paper
- Carrier bags
- Bills
- Receipts
- Order pads
- Empty packaging
- Food labels

These resources can be used in many ways to encourage the children to play, read and explore texts. Not only can these resources be used to create a bright and stimulating environment, they can also be used as resources for actual learning activities. Mail-order catalogues, for instance can really motivate children to use an index. Using laundry liquid bottles for measuring liquids can also lead to some letter and word recognition practice.

In addition to print from the environment beyond the classroom there is also the normal print common to all good early years settings. Labels on coat hooks and drawers, writing on displays, lists of words relating to topics, weather charts, registers, names and titles on workbooks and so on. Many of these are functional organisational features and yet they can all be used to the child's advantage. Putting away another child's book, changing the day of the week, looking at the register and so on are all further opportunities for children to use and explore print.

Reading and play

When children are playing they can be exploring, learning, practising and extending a whole range of skills and concepts. The quality of the learning which takes place during play can depend very much on the provision of support. The support comes in the form of play materials and resources, but also in the form of adult intervention. We have already considered how resources might be provided, particularly in role play corners, to invite children to read. Let us now focus on your interventions by reflecting on several questions about your own practice.

- Do you ever go into role to join the child's fantasy?
- How do you draw attention to print?
- How do you model yourself as a reader?
- How do you respond if the child 'pretend' reads?

- How do you respond if the child just 'reads' the illustrations?
- What sorts of questions do you ask children when they are playing?
- Why is it sometimes better to observe from a distance?
- Do you sometimes provide additional playthings to cater for unexpected developments?
- How do you show the children that play is a worthwhile activity?
- How do you extend the play ideas into other activities?

Many of the situations and activities described in this chapter will already have been familiar to you. However, we can all become so embroiled in the daily hustle and bustle of a busy workplace that sometimes things are taken for granted. The main message from this chapter is that almost every minute of the day provides excellent opportunities for developing children's reading in a wide variety of ways. These can be in addition to the planned discrete teaching of reading activities. Drawing attention to texts, letter and word recognition, reading for a purpose, booktalk and the sheer pleasure of stories and books all help to develop young children's reading strategies whilst at the same time giving them the implicit message that we regard them already as readers, that we respect their expertise and that we are firmly committed to extending that learning and development at every possible opportunity.

Notes for group leaders

⇨ Extend Activity 6.1 into a discussion in pairs taking turns to think of examples.

⇨ Display the games from Activity 6.3 for the whole group to see. Evaluate each other's games in pairs and give feedback.

⇨ Discuss the issues listed within the four categories of support.

⇨ In groups of six ask them to discuss their experiences of hearing children read. Who? When? How long? How often? Recording? Individual differences amd so on.

⇨ In groups of three look at a picture book then brainstorm follow-up activities across the curriculum.

⇨ In groups of four, brainstorm ideas for different role play corners and reading resources which could be provided for each.

Further reading

Baddeley, P. and Eddershaw, C. (1994). *Not So Simple Picture Books*. Stoke on Trent: Trentham Books.
Barr, M. and Thomas, A. (1991). *The Reading Book*. London: CLPE.
Brown, M. and Williams, A. (1995). *Eager Readers*. Oldham: Giant Steps.
Chambers, A. (1994). *Tell Me: Children Reading and Talking*. Stroud: Thimble Press.
Doonan, J. (1993). *Looking at Pictures in Picture Books*. Stroud: Thimble Press

CHAPTER 7

The developing writer

This chapter discusses the developmental nature of writing and how the experiences in early years settings can build usefully upon the early learning which has already taken place at home. It examines the processes of writing, the National Curriculum requirements, and the appropriateness of different types of adult support upon children's writing progress.

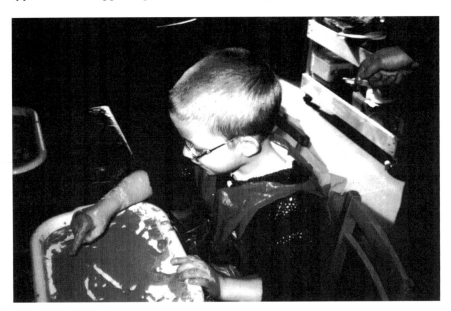

Writing can take place in a variety of media.

How does writing develop?

Throughout this book, reference has been made to the importance of enabling children to engage in language activities where oracy, reading and writing are integrated. Much of what has been said in the discrete chapters on oracy and reading apply equally to writing. By the time children start playgroup, nursery or school they have already accumulated a wealth of knowledge and understanding of the ways in which language works. They will be familiar with print within the social environment, and most will have had considerable experience of stories and books. In addition they will have experimented with writing and probably regard themselves as writers within their own world of play.

Basic concepts acquired are likely to include:

- print carries meaning
- print is different from pictures
- the words we say can be encoded into print
- print can be spoken out loud
- print written in English moves across the page from left to right
- print is composed of different units — letters, words, spaces, sentences etc.
- print comes in different shapes, colours and sizes
- writing is a meaningful activity
- adults write for many reasons
- adults read what other adults write

These concepts are so basic to experienced writers that adults can sometimes disregard them when accounting for what young children actually know, even though the concepts are built on significant experiences of texts, both as readers, writers and observers. However, if such concepts are to be utilised as sound foundations for the development of future learning the momentum and motivation of this pre-school writing should be maintained. Unfortunately, children can have quite misguided ideas about school 'work' and the expectations of teachers. It is quite common for children who are confident 'writers' at home and in nursery to become suddenly reluctant to write at school because they are afraid they might 'get it wrong'. So how can we ensure that the strong pre-school surge of writing motivation is not stemmed in its flow when the children embark upon more formal education?

Whilst recognising that children already have such competencies in writing when they start school, we must also acknowledge that children will be at different stages of writing development. Some will write fluently and confidently, some will write their own name, some will be unable to distinguish numbers from letters and so on. The first vital thing which adults working with young children need to understand is the developmental framework within which writing grows and changes. Approaches to writing which take this into account provide *continuity* for the child rather than presenting the child with a new and strange set of experiences which could undermine her confidence to learning.

There have been various useful models to demonstrate the stages of development in children's writing. Marie Clay (1975), through her careful and systematic observations of children's early writing, identified certain features which appear to be common to very young children.

☐ The recurring principle — repeated movements, e.g. loops

☐ The generative principle — small number of letters repeated in different combinations

☐ The sign concept — representational drawing, awareness that print carries message, e.g. McDonalds.

☐ The flexibility principle — invention of letters, knowledge of similarities between letters leads to experimentation

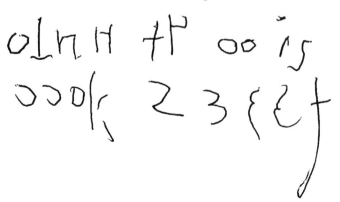

☐ Line and page principles —directionality, left-right, top-bottom, spaces between word,words as separate units

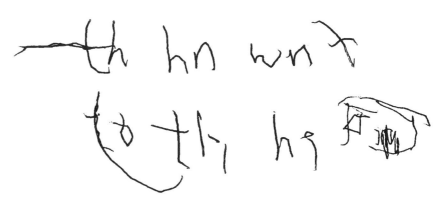

As with all developmental models, it is important not to regard such stages as independent units. There will always be overlap between phases as one merges into the other. However, what such models of developmental writing do help us with is the understanding that writing progresses —it changes. And those changes take place in a recognisable and sequential order. Recognition of the sequence enables us to define what the child has already learned and where they should be moving to next.

In Chapter 5, we looked at a model of reading in which the child moves from a supported role into independence. That same model is sometimes applied to writing, and is known as a 'developmental writing model'.

The stages of ➡ emergent ➡ supported ➡ fluent ➡ independent have been one useful way of regarding the developmental flow of writing, and the recognition of the early concepts mentioned at the beginning of this chapter are encompassed within the term 'emergent writer'. Children's perceptions of themselves as writers play an important role in their motivation and confidence to learn. To feel that they have no skills to offer can be extremely discouraging when they suddenly find themselves in a new and strange environment. The National Curriculum supports the principle of building on the emergent skills: 'Pupils' early experiments and independent attempts at communicating in writing, using letters and known words, should be encouraged'. (DFE, 1995).

However, as teachers continue to reflect on their own practice and the ways in which children approach writing, new theories of these stages will always continue to be discussed. One of the drawbacks with the previous model is that it fails to acknowledge that children can be very independent in their early writing. Indeed, it could be argued that certain forms of 'support', for example teachers' writing for children to copy, actually presents a barrier to children's learning and slows down the progression which has gone before. Insisting that the child should copy an adult's version of what the child wants to say has three main drawbacks:

1 The child all too often perceives this as a message that their writing is not good enough. In other words, that he or she is no longer regarded by others as a writer. This can affect confidence and limit the child's motivation to write independently.

2 The child is deprived of the opportunity to sound out and invent spellings — a process which plays a valuable part in the development of spelling.

3 The child is likely to be far less experimental in the things he or she plans to write and the vocabulary she is likely to attempt.

It is therefore helpful to use a developmental framework which recognises the child as an independent writer from the beginning and identifies the progressive features which should emerge as the child's writing develops. Such a model is represented below (Clipson-Boyles, 1996).

Developmental Stages of the Early Years Independent Writer

☐ *The emergent writer* understands the function of print and writes for different purposes in his or her play. This writing cannot normally be decoded by a reader unless they have observed the process and listened to the child's accompanying talk.

☐ *The exploratory writer* actively relates sounds to meaning through his or her own invented spellings. This writer is confident in his or her own ideas, perceives him- or herself as a writer and does not copy-write from an adult's writing above her own.

☐ *The communicative writer* writes texts which can be read by others. This writer seeks out, independently, letter and sound information from a range of sources, e.g. books, adults, other children, posters, word cards, displays. He or she will sometimes change words after they have been written.

☐ *The reflective writer* checks, reconsiders and redrafts his or her work. This redrafting is based on a recognition of the need for accuracy in punctuation, spelling and grammar. He or she is able to discuss his or her writing retrospectively and evaluates the effectiveness of his or her communication.

☐ *The versatile writer* is able to plan and adapt his or her style according to the purpose of and audience for the writing, and is able to move text around in order to reorganise his or her ideas when necessary. The majority of the writing is produced correctly, but ambitious use of extended vocabulary means that more challenging words are still misspelt. Editing and redrafting will take place in order to develop the quality of the work even further.

ACTIVITY 7.1 — Time: 30 minutes

With the permission of the teacher, make a collection of photocopies of children's writing and try to match the stages of development with one or more of the models discussed so far. For the Clipson-Boyles model you will also need to observe the children at work to check on the processes taking place.

Understanding the relationship between what children are already writing and where they need to go next is crucial if we are to nurture and nourish the pre-school shoots into healthy plants. However, it is also important to know what types of support are needed in order to ensure such growth. This can vary according to the context of the writing, and adult assistants should understand the different processes which can be involved with any writing activity if they are to make appropriate interventions.

The processes of writing

Imagine that you are looking at two stories written by seven year olds. One is in neatly joined handwriting, complete with full stops, capital letters and mostly correct spellings. The other is scrawled and untidy with evidence of many misspelt words. Your first impression might be that the first story is written at a higher level of competence than the second. Then, upon closer inspection, you note the following features:

Story 1 — short simple sentences, limited vocabulary, little description, muddled tenses, unclear storyline.

Story 2 — complex sentences with good use of conjunctions, misspelt words tend to be creative and adventurous vocabulary, storyline is well developed with good description of characters, mood and action.

How do we begin to assess which is the better piece of writing? The answer is that we can't make a general comparison between the two. We need to separate out the different components of the writing in order to see how each child is progressing within the different skill areas. Child 1 has a well developed style of handwriting, fluent, legible and presentable, but needs more work on sentence construction and use of vocabulary. Child 2 is a skilled story writer and an accomplished sculptor of words, but needs to develop more control over her handwriting. This hypothetical example is intended to illustrate the fact that when supporting children in their writing we need to be aware of the different processes which are involved.

Frank Smith (1982) divided these into two groups called 'authorship skills' and 'secretarial skills'. Authorship skills are about style, organisation, communication, development of ideas, creativity, adaptability to audience and purpose and sensitivity to the audience. Secretarial skills include spelling, punctuation, grammar and presentation.

The art of the supporting adult is to know when it is appropriate to intervene and why. Table 7.1 illustrates how it can be appropriate to offer certain types of support at different stages of the writing process.

Supporting children's spelling

Adults can sometimes have very unreasonable expectations of children's spellings — and their frustration shows when they try to correct a large percentage of a child's writing. Not only is this very discouraging to the child, it is also unrealistic to expect a child to digest such a vast amount of input learning in one go. Far better to prioritise fewer words which the child will learn most easily. One way of tuning in to where a child is at with their spelling is to relate it to a developmental framework for spelling.

Gentry (1987) proposes that children's spelling moves through five identifiable stages:

⇨ *precommunicative stage* where the child writes down random shapes and letters and numbers to represent meaning. This is unlikely to be legible to another reader.

Table 7.1 Stages of adult support during writing processes

Adult support for secretarial	Child's writing processes	Adult support for authorship
	Planning	← Stimulus provision
		← Encouraging discussion
	First draft	← Encourage independence
	Checking back	← Respond to meaning
		← Ask questions
		← Read together
	Re-drafting	← Encourage independence
Child checks spellings →		
Reads aloud for accuracy →	Correcting	
Evaluates presentation →		
Revise handwriting rules →	Final draft	← Reminder of purpose
Remember reader's needs →		

⇨ *semiphonetic stage* where the child represents whole chunks of sounds with single letters, e.g. fm = farm, tct = tractor

⇨ *phonetic stage* where the child introduces vowels and represents most of the sounds phonetically e.g. camru = camera, sestu = sister

⇨ transitional stage where the child starts to demonstrate a knowledge of spelling patterns and rules, e.g. trolly = trolley, powny = pony

⇨ *correct stage* where the child has a good understanding of spelling rules, can apply these to attempts at new words, and visualise and say spellings before writing them down.

This model is particularly helpful when assessing children's writing because it provides a clear diagnostic framework for teachers when they are planning a spelling programme. It also helps adults to decipher what children are writing and understand the level of their approach.

Spelling involves a complex set of brain processes. These include what we see, what we hear, what we remember and how we feel the directional movement of our pen. It is therefore appropriate that spelling is taught with these multi-sensory skills in mind, and teachers ususally employ a range of methods to help children to develop their spelling vocabulary.

Adults who are assisting children in their writing need to consider the following when providing additional support for spelling.

● Respect children's own attempts.

- Clap the rhythms of the words to idenify the syllables.
- Play and have fun with words and sounds.
- Note any patterns in their mistakes and prioritise what they need to learn next.
- Always encourage the child to have a go first before writing a word for them.
- Help the child to say the sounds aloud and think about the order of those sounds.
- Draw on the child's existing alphabet knowledge.
- Draw attention to the parts of words (chunks).
- Encourage the use of memory (look and cover).
- Practise the 'feel' of letter groups (linking with handwriting).
- Link writing to reading.
- Write three versions of a word for child to choose correct version.
- Make links with other similar words.
- Discourage dictionaries at the first draft stage.
- Encourage dictionaries at the redraft stage.
- Let child highlight words which need correcting — they ususaly do know.
- Explain that spotting mistakes isn't a sign of failure, it is a sign of success.
- Let the children see you using a dictionary sometimes — we all need them!

Handwriting

Schools generally recognise that handwriting should be taught correctly from an early stage and therefore will have a clearly defined handwriting policy. Habits, once formed, are very hard to change, so getting it right from the start is important. Supporting adults should ensure that they are familiar with this so that they are modelling the correct approach to letter formation and strokes. Handwriting is a motor skill which has to be taught and practised. It is such a physical part of the writing process that individual checking and support is usually needed. The following checklist is designed to help:

- Is the child sitting comfortably?
- Can the child see his or her paper?
- How is the child holding his or her pencil?
- Is the child leaving spaces between words?
- Is the child recognising the heights of tall and upper case letters?
- Are the letter formations in line with the school policy?

In addition, if the child is left-handed:

- Does the child have enough elbow room?
- Is the paper to the child's left, tilted slightly so he or she can see her writing?
- Are you demonstrating in a way which is possible with the left hand?
- Are you allowing the child enough time?

ACTIVITY 7.2 — Time: 5 minutes
Using Sheet 13 on page 84 make a copy of the text using the hand which you don't normally use for writing.

Play provides valuable contexts for writing.

Writing and play

Writing activities can have a very appropriate place within children's play activities, particularly if they represent a natural progression to the play as chosen by the child. Within a play context the child is usually in charge of the decision making and therefore the writing is driven by the child's will or need to write. However, the likelihood of the child making that choice is also dependent upon the resources available. If there is a message pad and pen by the telephone in the home corner he or she is far more likely to write a 'messsage' than if there is not. Many nurseries have a writing corner, where children can use the resources to write for any purpose they have identified — this might spring from other areas of play (e.g. making a bill for the car the child has just repaired) or might be a discrete writing activity (e.g. writing a story). Such writing corners work well where there is a variety of resources such as:

- different shapes of paper
- different coloured paper
- different sizes of paper
- scrap paper and best paper
- lined paper and plain paper
- envelopes
- bookmaking resources
- folders
- range of writing implements (including pens)
- pencil sharpeners
- rubbers
- stencils
- hole punchers
- labels
- typewriters
- post box

- words on display
- examples of texts
- dictionaries and thesauruses

Children should have free access to these resources but should also be taught how to use them correctly and leave the area tidy.

ACTIVITY 7.3 — Time: 10 minutes
Make a list of the types of writing opportunities which could be provide in six different role play corners.

Writing at the computer

Writing at the computer offers children excellent opportunities to link reading and writing. It also encourages children to edit easily, and produce a presentable piece of text. All children should have access to IT skills from an early age if they are to be prepared for the technological society in which we now live. When supporting children at the computer try to encourage them to:

- use all their fingers for typing
- use their thumbs for the space bar
- write first then edit
- print out and highlight corrections
- read back their own work
- store their work and come back to it later where appropriate

Computers provide valuable reading and writing opportunities for young children.

Writing across the curriculum

There are numerous opportunities for children to write in most areas of learning. This variety offers children the opportunity to write in different ways and for different reasons. Children are much more motivated to write when they:

- have a good reason for writing

- when they have something to write about
- when the writing is likely to illicit a response or reply
- have resources to stimulate their writing
- feel safe to experiment

Table 7.2 Types of writing across the curriculum

Activity	Curriculum area	Format
Collect mini-beasts draw	Science	Chart
Word games	Literature	Lists
Seasons word play	Science	Word collages
		List poems
		Shape poems
Clothes lists	Science	List
Weather recording	Geography/science	Diary
Bookmaking	Various	Books
Sequencing and writing	Various	Story
Cooking	Technology	Recipe card
Model making	Technology	Plan or list
Diagrams	Various	Labels
Messages to. . .	Language	Letters
Puppet plays	Language	Story scripts
Greetings cards	Language/RE	Card
Write to people in hospital	Topic	Letter
Instructions for a game	Various	Ordered list
Word trees	Various	One word per leaf
Recycling sorting	Science	Chart
Advertising/appeals	Various	Posters
Papermaking	Technology	Reporting
Class newspaper	Language	Ads, news, class
Joke book	Language	Page layout
Role play corner	Language/topic	Various
Sorting	Maths	Recording
Shape	Maths	Description

Many of these activities will be familiar to you and you will no doubt know many more. The potential list is endless!

Writing and the National Curriculum

The National Curriculum stresses the importance of this sort of *range* in children's writing. They should have opportunities to write in different ways for different reasons and for a variety of audiences. This includes writing in different formats and also in different styles. Confidence, fluency and accuracy are listed as key skills, and pupils should also be given opportunities to plan and review their writing. Punctuation, spelling and handwriting are each outlined in particular as are Standard English and knowledge about language.

ACTIVITY 7.4—Time: 20 minutes
On a piece of paper, make a list of the different purposes, audiences and forms for writing which you have observed in the settings where

you work. Which do you notice the children enjoying the most? Why?

Making the writing links with reading and speaking

Texts provide models for children's writing. The discussions you have with children when they are reading, about words, spaces, letters, full stops and so on are actively feeding in to their writing. Drawing attention to features in books and other texts is an important skill of the supporting adult. Every contact with a text is an opportunity to learn about writing.

When children are attempting their own spellings, saying and listening are crucial parts of the process. Sounding out the letters and blends, having fun with rhymes and distinguishing between the beginnings and endings of words are all helping to reinforce word construction skills.

Opportunities to collaborate

Collaborative writing is not just about writing in groups or pairs. It is also about the nature of the writing process. It is about not writing in isolation, but taking opportunities to consult in a range of ways.

Supporting children through discussing their writing.

The collaborative writer might consult:	in order to obtain:
pupils	feedback
teachers	advice
parents	information
other adults	ideas
editors	comment
books	
other resources	
previous work	
dictionaries	
thesaurus	
other texts	

This collaboration contributes to the learning benefits of the total process. Supporting adults can be there for consultation, but should also be aware of these other places where the children should be encouraged to seek out what they need. Actively encouraging children to make their own decisions about such collaboration makes an important contribution to children's developing thinking, confidence and independence.

Responses to writing

The ways in which you respond to children's writing will play an important part in what they attempt next. Different schools will have different approaches to the ways in which children's work is corrected, but for those who play a supporting role, the following guidelines provide a framework for response which is designed to assist learning.

- Respond to the content first.
- Show an interest in the writing.
- Ask the child about the subject matter.
- Ask the child what they think of the writing.
- Read the writing together.
- Praise the attempts at spellings before pointing out they are wrong.
- Do not overload the child with too many mistakes to think about (i.e. which is most appropriate for them to learn next?).
- Ask if the child would like to change or check anything.

Where possible, it is useful to write a response to the child. This enables the writing and reading to interlink in a very meaningful way but also enables you to model the spellings which the child has not yet learned. Figure 7.7 demonstrates how the adult has responded to the child's writing by showing interest, asking a question and also modelling some of the words which the child misspelt.

Responding and modelling

Giving children encouragement is not just designed to keep them happy. It is a way of ensuring that they will want to try again rather than feeling they have failed or are not capable of the task in hand. Encouragement can be given for different things:

- having a go
- using interesting words
- changing and correcting own writing
- checking a word
- experiment with new ideas
- taking the initiative
- reflecting on their own writing

ACTIVITY 7.5—Time: ongoing

Use Sheet 14 on page 85 to focus on aspects of your own practice. Do not overload yourself with too many questions at once! Wherever possible, discuss these with the teacher and where necessary list some action points on the back of the sheet. Plan to revisit these at a later date to monitor your progress.

Notes for group leaders

⇨ Ask the students to bring in the samples collected for Activity 7.1 and compare them. Discuss what certain children might need to learn next in terms of their writing.

⇨ Discuss Activity 7.2 to see how it felt. What are the implications for where the paper is positioned when two children are writing together?

⇨ As an extension of Activity 7.3, in pairs, plan and make writing resources for a role play corner.

⇨ Have a group discussion about the writing policies known to the group.

⇨ Asking the group to work as individuals set them a writing task under limited time conditions and with little or no stimulus or discussion. At the end, ask how they felt whilst writing, what else would they have liked to know, what would they like to happen to their writing next, etc.

⇨ Collect together samples of children's writing. Discuss the features and stages of development.

Further reading

Alston, J. (1995). *Assessing and Promoting Writing Skills*. Stafford: NASEN.

Browne, A. (1993). *Helping Children to Write*. London: Paul Chapman Publishing Ltd.

Clay, M. (1975). *What Did I Write?*: Auckland, NZ: Heinemam.

Cripps, C. and Cox, C. (1989). *Joining the ABC—How and why Handwriting and Spelling should be Taught Together*. Wisbech: Learning Development Aids.

DFE (1995). *English in the National Curriculum* ('The Order'). London: HMSO.

Gentry, J. (1987). SPEL is a four-letter word. Leamington Spa: Scholastic.

Hall, N.(ed.) (1989). *Writing With Reason*. London: Hodder & Stoughton.

Redfern, A. (1993). *Practical Ways to Teach Spelling*. Reading: The Reading and Information Centre.

Sassoon, R. (1990). *Handwriting; The Way to Teach It*. Bath: Leopard Learning.

CHAPTER 8

Supporting second language learners

Many children in the UK are learning English as their second language. Sadly, this is often regarded as an additional responsibility by some schools who are so used to the monolingual culture which results from living on an island. Yet in other developed countries of the world bilingualism and multilingualism are the norm. Indeed in some countries it is considered to be a considerable social disadvantage to speak, read and write only one language.

The language and literacy frameworks presented in this book provide good models of practice for supporting second-language learners. However, this chapter sets out to discuss some of the particular issues relating to bilingualism and biliteracy, and looks at some of the practical implications of providing effective support for, and enhancement of, a range of languages, including English, in early years settings.

Three basic truths for multilingual education

It is difficult, if not impossible, to separate out multilingual issues from the political and social agendas of our time. Whilst it is not the main purpose of this chapter to discuss multiculturalism, anti-racism and equal opportunities in great depth, it is important nevertheless to point out that the successful and healthy development of these areas are dependent on everything we do in early years settings.

The ways in which adults approach language and literacy in early years settings are ingrained with attitudes and implied messages. If we are to succeed in our mission to help children develop the necessary language skills we must develop a sound understanding and awareness of the fact that all we do and say has an impact upon all the children in our care. Bearing that in mind, there are three basic truths which should be central to our practice.

Truth Number 1. The linguistic needs of second language learners require both languages to be respected, valued and used in their learning.

Research (Cummins, 1994) and projects (Multilingual Resources for Children Project, 1995) have demonstrated that helping children to be confident in their own language gives them a firmer foundation upon which to build the learning of their second language. In other words there are sound linguistic reasons for not excluding the home language from the educational setting.

Truth Number 2. The social and psychological needs of second language learners require both languages to be respected, valued and used in their learning.

Our language is part of our identity. To forbid or discourage children to use their home and community language can undermine their confidence and self esteem. It is also giving an insidious message of the superiority of English over their own language. This tension between the two languages can lead to conflict and confusion. Alternatively, to demonstrate to children that their language is valued and respected can provide a positive approach to learning the two languages side by side.

Truth Number 3. The linguistic, social and psychological needs of monolingual English speakers require a variety of languages to be respected, valued and used in their learning.

The Cox Report (DES, 1988) recommended that one of the ways children should learn language is through learning *about* language. This is commonly referred to now as KAL (Knowledge About Language). Exploring the diversity of languages, accents and dialects, including Standard English, can help children to develop their knowledge and understanding of how language works. The multilingual setting offers a rich resource for learning not only about languages and texts, but also about how to build a mutually rewarding partnership with children from different cultural backgrounds. Such learning is important for all monolingual English-speaking children, regardless of the cultural mix in their community.

ACTIVITY 8.1 — Time: ongoing
Before embarking upon this activity you will need to consult with you teacher mentor and your headteacher or whoever is in charge of your workplace. Using a copy of Sheet 15 on page 86 make a careful record of the language knowledge of eight children. If there are no bilingual or multilingual children available to you it will still be interesting to see what awareness and knowledge even young monolinguals have of other languages.

What do I need to know about languages?

All adults working with young children have a responsibility to acquire a certain knowledge of the languages and backgrounds of those children. This does not mean becoming fluent in all the languages you are likely to encounter! That would be unrealistic. But to learn a few simple words, particularly greetings, gives a strong message that you are not only interested, but also approving and accepting. Involving the child in teaching you (and the other children) more about their language is also a valuable way into discussion about language skills.

Other areas you might need to explore include:

● Do both parents speak the same language?
● Is the home language also a community language?
● Is the spoken language the same as the written?
● In which direction does the written text travel?

- Is there a special language for the purposes of religion?
- Is the child educated by other educators (e.g. community language teachers)?

It is also helpful to understand common language terminology. The following words are often used to talk about language.

accent	– variation in pronunciation
bilingual	– regularly uses two languages to speak
biliterate	– able to read and write in two languages
dialect	– variations in grammatical structure/vocabulary
monolingual	– speaks in one language proficiently
multilingual	– three or more languages (not necessarily proficient)
TEFL	– Teaching English as a Foreign Language
ESL	– English as a Second Language
TESOL	– Teaching English to speakers of other languages

In this chapter, the term 'multilingual setting' is used to refer to a place where there are three or more languages, including English, spoken by different children.

ACTIVITY 8.2 — Time: 90 minutes
Go to your local library and find out what are the most common languages spoken in your county using council information. Then, using books from the library make a copy of the words 'Welcome' or 'Greetings' in as many different scripts as you can find. Ask the librarians where else you can go to find out more about particular languages which are spoken in your area.

Sharing dual text books offers a rich source of discussion and interest.

Should bilingual children work on their own? Language exists in order for us to communicate. Children cannot communicate alone. Throughout this book, the integrated nature of language has been discussed. The links between speaking, listening, reading and writing are a natural and constructive part of children's language learning. These processes are interactive and require exchanges with others. Bilingual children benefit enormously from working in English-speaking groups because it gives them opportunities to:

- listen to the sounds of English
- observe the exchanges of others
- practise responding in English
- ask questions
- answer questions
- repeat what they hear
- use body language for clues
- receive support from other children

Working in a pair with a child who speaks the same home language offers bilingual children opportunities to:

- consolidate ideas
- clarify areas of uncertainty
- answer questions
- translate
- develop confidence in their learning

Working in a pair with a child who speaks English offers both children opportunities to:

- write dual texts
- discuss and translate
- listen to both languages
- speak both languages
- teach each other about their languages

Working with an English-speaking supporting adult offers bilingual children opportunities to:

- share their worries
- ask questions in English
- answer questions in English
- repeat and practise
- revisit previous learning
- talk about their home language
- 'teach' the adult
- enjoy looking at books
- observe writing

Working with a supporting adult who speaks the child's home language offers that child opportunities to do all the things in the previous list plus:

- develop their home language;
- learn to switch between languages;
- listen to ideas explained in their own language;
- have instructions translated;
- answer questions in their own language;
- ask questions in their own language; and

- conceptualise ideas in their own language.

Working on their own bilingual children have the opportunity to:

- do very little to further their language development. . .

ACTIVITY 8.3 — Time: 30 minutes

Using Sheet 16 on page 91 make a record of your observations of bilingual children working in groups. If you do not have the opportunity to observe bilinguals in your own workplace, it would be well worth making your own arrangements to visit somewhere else where there will be more children to observe. Explain and discuss your task with those who are in charge so that they can agree to the activity and perhaps even offer you advice about which children to observe. The sheet describes the observation process in more detail.

What types of learning experiences are particularly beneficial to bilingual learners?

The interactive contexts mentioned above can operate right across the curriculum. Activities which are particularly useful to language learners are:

Bookmaking	Storytelling and technology create an active learning situation in which children can talk, listen, write, read, make and draw.
Booktalk	Sharing picture books enables the bilingual child to listen, say and look. The pictures provide a strong context for the child to make meaning. Books with a cumulative repeated pattern are also useful for enjoyable practice, as are rhyming and rhythmic verse. Books which have a box of related artefacts are particularly useful. Making storyboxes can also be fun for the children.
Storytelling	Telling known stories, new stories or stories about oneself — the ancient art of storytelling is central to human existence and is a completely cross-cultural activity, as natural as talk itself!
Re-telling	Right across the curriculum, the opportunity to re-tell reaps rich rewards for bilingual learners. Artefacts can serve a useful purpose in reminding the child as they re-tell. These could range from the seeds which have just been planted, to the clothes to be put on after PE.
Drama/Role play	'Playing' the roles of others help children to explore and experiment with a range of language for a variety of purposes.
Puppets	Designing and making puppets is fun, but to use them is even better. Links with storymaking and technology again make this a dynamic hands-on activity with a lot of purposeful communication.
Masks	A mask can help to give a child the confidence to speak because they have a shield. They can also become someone else. Characters from stories can be a powerful

66

	voice for a child to use when developing confidence in spoken language.
Photographs	Photographs of the children, their families and other related subjects can be a tremendously stimulating resource for young children. They can be used for discussion, displays, art activities and bookmaking.
Cooking	Nothing motivates children quite like cooking, except perhaps eating! Cooking provides particularly good opportunities to explore cultural variety in an exciting and experiential way. Do beware of introducing stereotypes. Seeing a British-Chinese father cook Lancashire hotpot could do wonders for breaking down barriers!
Visitors	A visitor is a focus for attention, whether that visitor is a newborn baby or the local vet. Listening and questioning have a real context when appropriate people visit an early years setting, and the activity provides an opportunity to broaden the variety of role models for the children.
Visits	Educational visits do not have to take all day and needn't cost anything. The local area will always provide a good range of resources to stimulate children's language, and provide excellent starting points for learning by building on what the children know well.
Festivals	Festivals provide a starting point for a wide range of cross-curricular and discrete language development work. These should be explored meaningfully rather than through token reference.
Play	All play activities provide opportunities for language development. The talk which takes place during play can be an important mechanism for allowing children to organise their thoughts. Toys give children additional cues for their spoken language.
Writing corners	A writing area which is resourced with a wide range of writing implements, different types, sizes, colours and shapes of paper and displays of different types of texts can be very inviting to children if they are encouraged and rewarded for their efforts.
Listening corners	Listening to story tapes with a book is a popular activity for all children. Tapes can also be used for games, instructions and repeating an activity. It is very rewarding for children to make their own tapes in addition to using commercial tapes.
Computers	Programmes with a high graphic input alongside the text are invaluable to bilingual learners. Multimedia systems (though few schools can afford these at the moment) are of particular benefit as they also incorporate sound and therefore completely interactive.

Support should be offered in the home language as well as English.

How useful are dual-text books?

Dual language texts have been well received by teachers and pupils in Britain since the mid-1980s. They offer all children the opportunity to examine and learn about another language, whilst at the same time supporting children who are learning English as a second language. Indeed, dual language texts can be used in a variety of useful ways.

However, they do vary so much in quality that it is important for adults in early years settings to develop a critical awareness of these books in order to enhance their use and, where appropriate, influence purchasing decisions. The following activity is designed to help you focus your attention on a dual language text in a way which critically evaluates the book.

- Which language comes first?
- Does one language have more prominence on the page?
- Are both languages written in the same size?
- Does each language have equal status?
- How has the inclusion of two texts affected the page layout?
- If one language is required to run in a different direction to English what effect does this have on the reader?
- How will the book be read?
- Are the pictures useful to the reader?
- Is the author English?

- Is the story from the culture of the home language?

Dual language labels help bilingual children but are also interesting to all children.

Single-language texts

It is appropriate and educationally sound to provide children with texts written in their home language in addition to solely English texts and dual language texts. Not only does it help to build the sound foundations of language and literacy in the home language, it helps to develop and maintain a sense of cultural ownership of those stories. To deprive children of stories and authors from their own cultures is to deprive them of a valuable part of their developing sense of self and can also affect their language development.

What qualities of support can I offer bilingual children?

Many of the qualities which you already offer when supporting children's learning will be appropriate and helpful to bilingual children. In addition you also need to consider the following:

- Do not patronise. These children are language experts!
- Tune in to what the child knows.
- Take an interest in their language.
- Take an interest in their culture.
- Ask them to teach you some words.
- Try to link sounds to images.
- Use artefacts when explaining.
- Draw when explaining.
- Use artefacts when reading and telling stories.
- Make good use of pictures when using books.
- Include pictures in all writing activities.
- Use lots of body language to enhance meaning.
- Repeat what you have said often.
- Ask the child to repeat what you have said often.

- Ask the child to re-tell what others (e.g. teacher) have said.
- Be a good listener.
- Learn from what you hear.
- Correct mistakes by being a role model rather than a critic.

Notes for group leaders   ⇨   Sharing experiences through discussion will be particularly important for this topic as there is likely to be a wide range of views and experiences.

⇨   Wherever possible, Activities 8.1 and 8.3 should be planned and discussed with a mentor, or a training colleague.

⇨   Additional group activities could include:
- puppet making
- collecting artefacts for a story
- designing a role-play corner
- making dual text books
- making books with photographs
- making dual text labels and signs

Further reading

DES (1985). *Education For All.* (The Swann Report).London:HMSO.

Edwards, V. (1995). *Reading in Multilingual Classrooms.* Reading: Reading and Language Information Centre.

Edwards, V. (1995). *Speaking and Listening in Multilingual Classrooms.* Reading: Reading and Language Information Centre.

Edwards, V. (1995). *Writing in Multilingual Classrooms.* Reading: Reading and Language Information Centre.

ILEA (1988). *The Primary Language Record.* London: Centre for Language in Primary Education.

Multilingual Resources for Children Project (1995). *Building Bridges: Multilingual Resources for Children.* Reading: Reading and Language Information Centre.

Activity Sheets

The sheets on the following 12 pages may be photocopied for use in activities and study. This includes the reproduction of more than one copy by purchasing institutions for educational purposes within that institution only.

SHEET 1

Reflecting on yourself in a working partnerships

Think about your main current working partnership. If you are not currently employed, try to recall a partnership from a previous post, or with a fellow trainee.

What qualities do you think you bring to this partnership?

What qualities does the other person bring to the partnership?

What is the worst problem you have encountered in this partnership?

How did you deal with this?

In retrospect, how would you like you deal with it differently if that was possible?

How do you usually respond to criticism from other people?

Think of an area of your work to criticise. Make a negative statement about it here as if it was being said by someone else!.

Try to think of a creative response to the criticism, perhaps identifying three action points to follow.

Now try to find someone with whom you can discuss your responses to this activity. Decide first what you want to gain from the discussion. . .

Developing team skills

Tick the boxes where you feel confident about your ability. Then look at the unticked boxes. Try to use these constructively by using them in the following way:

- make notes for yourself
- talk to others
- observe others
- set yourself realistic goals
- write down what you would like to aim for
- re-evaluate yourself in six months time

1. Belief system
- Am I committed to the overall success of the team?
- Do I expect my team leader to take all responsibility?
- Do I have high expectations of the team's work?

2. Self-awareness
- What are my own strengths and skills?
- What are my own limitations?
- What is my role within the group?
- When should I ask for help and advice?

3. Social skills
- Do I support the needs of others?
- Am I a good listener?
- What impact do I have on others?
- Do I avoid problems?
- Am I committed to exploring conflict and resolving difficulties?
- Do I recognise the importance of honest relationships?
- Do I respect the feelings of others?
- Do I respect different viewpoints?
- Do I know when it is appropriate to speak up?
- Do I know when it is more useful to keep quiet?

4. Professional skills
- Do I take advice constructively?
- Do I give advice constructively?
- Do I communicate clearly?
- Do I work with and not against others?
- How do I think creatively?
- How do I demonstrate flexibility?
- How do I share the responsibility of decision making?
- Am I clear about my role but not inflexible?
- Can I work independently without undermining the work of the team?
- Do I reflect and build continuously on my performance and practice?

Variety in language

Choose three of the language communities listed in Figure 2.1 in Chapter 2. In the three sections below list the differences between them by thinking about: (a) vocabulary and (b)purposes

An example has been completed for you.

SITUATION: visit to the seaside

VOCABULARY	**PURPOSES**
sand, sea, bucket, spade, seagull, hotel, visitors, costumes, jet-ski etc	asking about new experiences asking for treats describing new sights describing emotions 'reading' attractions posters

SITUATION:

VOCABULARY	**PURPOSES**

SITUATION:

VOCABULARY	**PURPOSES**

SITUATION:

VOCABULARY	**PURPOSES**

SHEET 4

Play and language

Observation record

Child: _____ Date: _____

Activity: _____

Description of actions, spoken language and interactions with texts

SHEET 5

Child observations

In a pair
Date: _____ **Context:**

In a small group (e.g. 3 or 4)
Date: _____ **Context:**

Whole class situation (eg storytime)
Date: _____ **Context:**

One-to-one with an adult
Date: _____ **Context:**

SHEET 6

Self-evaluation

Context: _____

Number of children: _____

How did I introduce the activity?

What sorts of questions did I ask?

What sorts of questions did the children ask?

How did I find out what they already knew?

How do I know what each child had learned by the end?

What might I do differently if I could repeat this activity?

Analysing your own talk

Think back to when you woke up yesterday and imagine that your day was recorded on video! In the first two columns below, record as much of the talk as you can remember by mentally recalling the order of events and the people to whom you spoke. It might help to do this chronologically.

Next, try to examine each example more closely by listing the reason for your talk and the type of talk which you consider it to be. Two examples have been given to guide you.

Situation	Person	Example	Type of talk
In bed	Son	Shouted to get him to turn his music down!	Command
Telephone	BT clerk	Complain about bill	Complaint questions

Thinking about your talk with children

The following questions are designed to help you to reflect on your own practice. Every day we talk automatically, sometimes without thinking about what we say and how we say it. A closer, critical examination of that talk can be useful and sometimes surprising.

- When starting a group activity do you give the pupils chance to talk about what they already know?

- When you explain something do you give the children chance to ask questions?

- When you give instructions how do you know they are clear?

- When you ask questions is there always only one answer?

- Do your questions open up possibilities for discussion?

- Do you allow the children to bring in their own ideas and experience where appropriate even if this takes you away from the original point?

- How do you show children that you are listening?

- How do you show children that you value their contributions?

- If a child offers a totally wrong answer how do you tell them so that they do not feel embarrassed or discouraged?

- What is the balance between your talk and that of the pupils?

- How do you decide when pupil talk is off-task?

- What techniques do you use to move the talk back on-task?

- Is a reprimand always an effective way to do this?

- How can your attitude towards the children help to improve their listening skills?

- In a whole class situation, how might you involve those pupils who are 'on the fringe'?

ACTION POINTS:

SHEET 9

What do I do when I read?

On the chart below, make notes about how you read the different types of text listed.

Text	What do I do when I read this?
Magazine	
Telephone directory	
Recipe	
Newspaper	
Junk mail	
Party political leaflets	
Personal letter	
Written feedback	
TV guide	
Special offers	

Analysing your reading strategies

Below you will find four unusual examples of text. Cover these up immediately without looking at them. One at a time, uncover the texts and try to read them. Make notes after each one of the strategies you have used to decipher and understand what is written.

Text 1

The fat cat was too large to squeeze through the cat flap.

Text 2

Lxst wxxk I vxsxtxed my mxthxr xnd fxthxr. I dxdnt knxw thxt my sxstxr wxs xlsx gxxng tx bx thxrx. Wx hxd x gxxd chxt bxcxxsx wx hxdnt sxxn xxch xthxr fxr x lxng txmx.

Text 3

viss iss u spilink lisst ken u reid ve wudz buk knighs trea soopa pownd phinnish throo seeling benniffitt skweez schoopeed owver reesint bredd

---

Text 4

Little Rid Reding Hood was unsure about which path she should take. The volvo was chasing her down one path and the mad woodkiller was down the other. If only she could reach her granddaughter's house. Then she would be quiet safe. The sound of the volvo's engine revving became louder and louder. The woodpecker's cries were blood-curdling. There was only one thing left to do. She must find the mobile home and phone her mother.

SHEET 11

Getting to know a reader

Please consult with the teacher before doing this task. It is important that you choose the child together and that no unusual pressure or demands are placed upon that child. The activity is intended to strengthen your understanding of what is happening when children read so that you can provide appropriate support.

CHILD: _____ DATE: _____

BOOK: _____

Child's attitudes to reading

Child's attitudes to books

What does the child know already about books?
    Author
    Title
    Pages
    Front/back
    Left to right
    Top to bottom
    Words
    Letters
    Spaces
    Full stops

Words that caused problems on this occasion

Letters that caused a problem on this occasion

Word attack skills

Use of contextual clues

Memory of story

Discussion of own experiences relating to story

SHEET 12

Supporting reading across the curriculum

Consider the following situations in a nursery and jot down ideas for resources and types of adult intervention which might support and develop aspects of a child's reading.

Situation	Resources	Intervention
Sand tray		
Water tray		
Home corner		
Role play office		
Writing corner		
Technology workshop		
Making displays		
Cooking		
Planting seeds		
Local walk		
Using plasticine		
Computer		

3

Handwriting

This task is designed to help you understand how a child feels when they are learning to write. Using the hand which you do not normally use for writing, make a copy of the text on the top half of the page by writing on the bottom half of the page. Make a note of how it feels and of any changes you needed to make in order to compensate.

Why did Mr. Fish (an acquaintance of George Bernard Shaw) like to spell his name in a more interesting way?

Mr. GHOTIUGH
GH = f as in tough
O= i as in women
TI= sh as in initial
UGH= silent as in though

YOUR COPY...

84

Reflecting on your own practices

During the course of one week, try to focus on one question at a time. Use the process to identify any areas in which you might like to seek further advice from the teacher. Make a list of action points on the back of a photocopy of this sheet.

- When a child asks you for a spelling what other things can you do to encourage independence and confidence?

- When do you ask children to read their writing to you?

- How do you respond to the content of children's writing?

- Do you point out the mistakes before you find the good elements?

- How do you point out mistakes?

- How might you encourage the child to discuss other ideas of their own?

- How do you suggest new ideas to the child without taking over the ownership of the work?

- How do you show children that you value their contributions?

- If a child offers a totally wrong answer how do you tell them so that they do not feel embarrassed or discouraged?

- How can you set mini-targets to help a child through a much larger task?

- When children are practising handwriting do you observe the strokes?

Recording children's knowledge of languages in addition to English

This activity is a mini-survey of children's knowledge of other languages in addition to English. Such a record was first pioneered in London using *The Primary Language Record* (ILEA, 1988) and was found to be an invaluable way of gaining insight into the breadth of children's language knowledge.

In consultation with your teacher-mentor and headteacher, or whoever is in charge of your workplace, choose eight children for the survey. If possible try to include children who you know are bilingual or multilingual. If you can talk to the children's parents as well as the children you will gain a much broader view of the language repertoire of your group.

NAME: **UNDERSTANDS:**   **SPEAKS:**   **READS:**   **WRITES:**

SHEET 16

Bilingual group observations

Having received the approval of the person in charge, try to conduct a range of five-minute observations of bilingual children working in groups of different sizes, including pairs. It is advisable to use a fresh copy of this sheet for each situation you observe. The schedule below is designed to make your recording easier, but do go ahead and design a different format based on your own ideas if you wish.

Try to observe from a distance, otherwise you will be drawn into the activity! If it is possible and appropriate, a tape recorder could be placed close to the children as a back-up. In this case it is only fair to explain to the children that you are interested in their talk but that you want them to ignore the taping. They will probably enjoy listening to the tape themselves afterwards.

As you observe, note down the type of talk for each child as it happens using the following codes : E = explaining, Q = questioning, A = answering, R = repeating, D = describing . At the end your entries might look like this:

CHILD A   EEEQAAAAAA

If they used their home language, place a circle round the letter.

ACTIVITY AREA:

RESOURCES:

HOME LANGUAGE: CHILD A   CHILD B
                        CHILD C   CHILD D
                        CHILD E   CHILD F

A

B

C

D

E

F

When your observations are completed, look at them carefully and note any patterns or differences between the different situations. Make a list of four points which you feel might influence your future practice as a result of conducting this exercise.

References

Clay, M.M. (1975) *What Did I Write?* Auckland: Heinemann Educational Books

Clipson-Boyles, S.B. (1996) *Early Years Writing Stages*. Oxford: O.B.U. School of Education.

Cummins, J. (1994) The acquisition of English as a second language. In K.Sprangen-Urbschat and R. Pritchard (eds) *Kids Come in All Languages*, pp. 36–62. New Delaware: IRA.

Department of Education and Science (1988) *English for Ages 5–16* (The Cox Report). London: HMSO.

Department of Education and Science (1990) *Starting with Quality: Report of the Committee of Inquiry into the Educational Experiences Offered to Three and Four- Year Olds* (Rumbold Report), London: HMSO.

Department of Employment and Department of Education and Science (1986) *Working Together: Education and Training*. London: HMSO.

Department for Education (1995) *English in the National Curriculum*. London: HMSO.

Gentry, J.R. *Spel... is a Four-Letter Word*. Leamington Spa: Scholastic.

ILEA (1988) *The Primary Language Record*. London: CLPE.

Multilingual Resources for Children Project (1995) *Building Bridges: Multilingual Resources for Children*. Reading: Reading and Language Information Centre.

SCAA, TTA and ACAC (1996) *A Guide to the National Curriculum*. London: HMSO

Siraj-Blatchford, I (1992) Why understanding cultural differences is not enough. In Pugh, G. (ed) *Contemporary Issues in the Early Years—Working Collaboratively for Children*, pp. 104–121. London: NCB and Paul Chapman Publishing Ltd.

Smith, F. (1982) *Writing and the Writer*. Oxford: Heinemann.

Vygotsky, L.S. (1978) *Mind in Society: The Development of Higher Psychological Processes*. Cambridge, USA: Harvard University Press.

Wells, G. (1985) *Language, Learning and Education*. Windsor: NFER-Nelson.